Exploring
Marin Trails

by

Tacy Dunham

Have Fun Tacy

🌿 Cottonwood Press, California

Inquiries may be made to:

 Cottonwood Press
610 El Arroyo Place
Novato, CA 94949
(415) 382-8590
cottonwoodpress4ca@hotmail.com

ISBN# 1-877967-08-4

Cover Design: Keith Whitaker
Interior Design and Maps: Tacy Dunham
Copy Editor: Molly Roth
Cover photo: Mt. Tamalpais by Tacy Dunham
Illustration: Muir Woods by Troy Dunham
Back cover photos:
        Poppies: Troy Dunham
        Waterfalls in Steep Ravine: Troy Dunham
        Bon Tempe Lake: Tacy Dunham

Printed in the United States of America
using soy based inks on chlorine-free recycled paper.

West Coast Print Center
Oakland, California

This book is for
everyone who believes that walking in nature
is time well spent

My vicinity affords many good walks; and though for so
many years I have walked almost every day, and some-
times for several days together, I have not yet exhausted
them. An absolutely new prospect is a great happiness,
and I can still get this any afternoon.

from *Walking* by Henry David Thoreau

Trail Hints and Regulations

Trail Hints

Carry water and extra food.
Carry a map or trail book.
Wear sun protection, sunscreen, hat, long sleeves.
Take a jacket or windbreaker; Marin weather is changeable.
Carry a small first aid kit and a whistle.
Use good judgment in choosing trails.
Never short cut or go "cross country."
Recognize and avoid poison oak.
Carry out all trash.
Do not hike alone.
Tell someone where you're going and when you expect
    to return.

Regulations

No open fires.
No smoking May 1 to October 31 on open-space lands.
Camp only at designated areas.
Watershed lands are open only during daylight hours.
Obey closures during times of extreme fire danger.
Keep dogs on leash and on designated trails only.
Do not pick plants or flowers.
No collecting. All artifacts are protected by law.
Mountain bikes go on fire roads and designated trails only.
Horses must stay on designated trails.
Valid state license is required for fishing.
No motor vehicles.
No hunting or shooting.

Introduction

This book provides information about trails on Mt. Tamalpais, Marin Municipal Water District lands, Marin Open Space, Muir Woods National Monument, Angel Island State Park, China Camp State Park, Samuel P. Taylor State Park, Olompali State Historic Park, and McInnis County Park. This book will help you to locate trails and decide which hikes are best suited to your hiking ability. Every type of terrain is represented, from easy walks along level paths to challenging climbs up mountain ridges. Come and explore Marin trails.

How to use this book:
This guide presents 44 areas of exploration throughout Central Marin. Each map shows one or more recommended hikes.

Access:
You may need a street map of the cities of Marin County to help you locate some of the access points. Access points and parking availability are marked.

Difficulty of hike:
Easy: level or nearly level walking
Moderate: uphill grades on trails
Strenuous: steep sections on trails

Trail descriptions:
Brief descriptions of the trails are provided as a general guide to terrain. Notes on views, flora, fauna, and historical points are also included.

Disclaimer:
Use of trails and fire roads are at the user's own risk. The author can not accept liability or legal responsibility for trail changes, injuries, damage, or loss of direction or time resulting from use of information in this book. For the most current information and trail conditions, call the information telephone numbers provided.

MARIN COUNTY

Trail locations

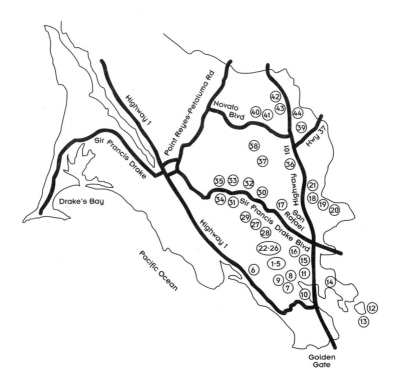

The numbers on this Marin County map show
the locations of the 44 trails listed in the
Table of Contents on the following page.

CONTENTS

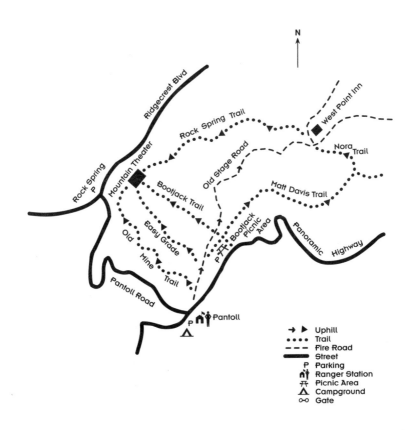

Legend:
- → ▶ Uphill
- •••• Trail
- – – – Fire Road
- ▬▬ Street
- P Parking
- ♀♂ Ranger Station
- 🎋 Picnic Area
- △ Campground
- o–o Gate

Easy Grade
Mt. Tamalpais State Park

ACCESS: Panoramic Highway

POINTS OF INTEREST: Historic sites, views, wildflowers

DISTANCE: Easy Grade–Old Mine loop: 2 miles
             Matt Davis–Nora–Rock Spring–Bootjack: 4.5 miles

DIFFICULTY: Moderate

INFORMATION: Mt. Tamalpais State Park
                     (415) 388-2070

Easy Grade
Mt. Tamalpais State Park

Easy Grade is an easy hike with lots to see, and it provides a good introduction to the trails on Mt. Tamalpais. The Easy Grade Trail–Old Mine Trail loop from Pantoll Ranger Station to the Mountain Theater is a 2-mile hike.

Beginning at the Pantoll Ranger Station, follow the Old Stage Road and turn off onto the Easy Grade Trail. This well graded footpath winds through a shady forest as it climbs 600 feet in elevation to the Mountain Theater. The theater began as a huge natural amphitheater where the first Mountain Play was staged on May 4, 1913. The massive 3,750-seat theater was built of local stone in the 1930s by the Civilian Conservation Corps. When you're ready to head down, locate the Old Mine Trail behind the restrooms and follow its zigzags down the ridge and enjoy views along the way.

For a longer loop, the Matt Davis, Nora, Rock Spring, and Bootjack trails combine to make a 4.5-mile trek that includes a visit to the West Point Inn and the Mountain Theater.

Begin at the Boot Jack Picnic Area and follow the trail sign to the Matt Davis Trail. This narrow footpath winds along the contour of the mountain with little elevation change. The trail traverses a variety of landscapes. At the trail junction, turn left and head up the Nora Trail. This short trail follows a creek up a ravine crowded with redwood trees and emerges from the woods at the West Point Inn. You can enjoy your lunch at the picnic tables or on the porch of this historic inn. The view over the Marin Headlands toward San Francisco is breathtaking.

The West Point Inn got its name from its location. It was the farthest point west on the railroad line that wound up to Mt. Tam's summit. This was the point were passengers traveling to Bolinas or Willow Camp (today's Stinson Beach) disembarked from the train and caught the stage. From 1913 through 1933, passengers going to the Mountain Play got off the train at the West Point Inn and walked the remaining mile to the Mountain Theater.

Continue your loop hike by following the Rock Spring Trail to the Mountain Theater and heading down the Bootjack Trail to the Boot Jack Picnic Area and parking lot.

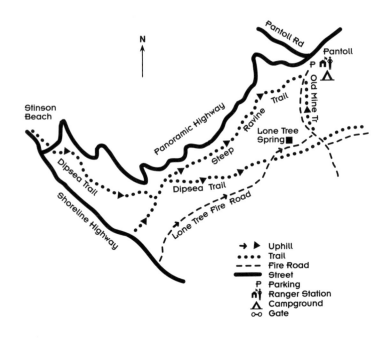

Steep Ravine
Mt. Tamalpais State Park

ACCESS: Panoramic Highway

POINTS OF INTEREST: Views, wildflowers, waterfalls

DISTANCE: Old Mine–Dipsea–Steep Ravine: 4 miles
Pantoll Ranger Station to Stinson Beach via
Steep Ravine and Dipsea: 3 miles

DIFFICULTY: Strenuous

INFORMATION: Mt. Tamalpais State Park
(415) 388-2070

Steep Ravine
Mt. Tamalpais State Park

The Steep Ravine Trail is a challenging hike along a stream with countless waterfalls and one of the most beautiful footpaths on Mt. Tamalpais. Combining the Old Mine, Dipsea, and Steep Ravine trails creates a 4-mile, strenuous loop that includes an uphill climb through Steep Ravine.

From the Pantoll parking lot, follow the Old Mine Trail through a forest of Douglas fir trees. The trail merges with a fire road a short distance before emerging from the trees onto an open ridge. On exceptionally clear days, you can see the clock tower on the UC Berkeley campus to the east, the blimp hangars at Moffit Field to the south, and the Farallon Islands to the west.

Join the Dipsea Trail or walk on the Lone Tree Fire Road which parallels it. You may want to make a brief stop at Lone Tree Spring in a cluster of redwood trees beside the fire road. The beautiful stonework at the spring was built by the Tamalpais Conservation Club in 1917.

Stay on the Dipsea Trail as it crosses the open ridge, then leaves the ridge crest and heads down into the ravine through a forest of bay trees thick with ferns. At the footbridge that crosses over Webb Creek, you may want to stop and enjoy the cool stream setting before you turn right and begin the climb.

As you hike up Steep Ravine's well-maintained path, notice the stone steps, wooden steps, handrails, and the ladder–its most famous feature. This is one of Mt. Tam's classic old trails, and keeping it open has been a labor of love for generations. Individuals as well as clubs, the Conservation Corps, and park staff all deserve credit for maintaining this popular footpath.

Webb Creek tumbles down the deeply carved ravine. Cascades thunder as the stream rushes through the boulder-strewn hillside and drops into crystal pools. Adding to the wild character of the gorge are downed redwood trees. Like enormous pick-up sticks, shattered tree trunks span the ravine. Amid the jungle-like atmosphere of huge ferns and lush vegetation, spring and summer wildflowers create a parade of botanical color and texture that adds delicate beauty to an otherwise wild scene.

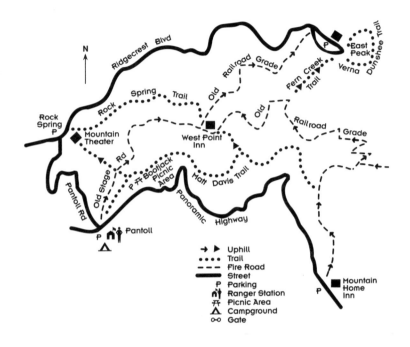

Mt. Tam Summit
Mt. Tamalpais State Park

ACCESS: Panoramic Highway or Ridgecrest Blvd.

POINTS OF INTEREST: Views, wildflowers, historic sites

DISTANCE: Verna Dunshee Trail: .7 miles, easy
Old Stage Road–Old Railroad Grade: 7.5 miles,
moderate

DIFFICULTY: Easy, Moderate

INFORMATION: Mt. Tamalpais State Park
(415) 388-2070

Mt. Tam Summit
Mt. Tamalpais State Park

A drive up to the summit of Mt. Tamalpais is one of the finest day trips Marin has to offer. The Verna Dunshee Trail circles the summit. This easy, .7-mile walk features marvelous views. A portion of trail is wheelchair accessible. There is a picnic area near the parking lot and a small visitor's center.

As you begin your circle of the summit, you can see the ridges of the Marin Headlands to the south. Look closely and you can also see one orange tower of the Golden Gate Bridge, with San Francisco in the background. To the east, Mt. Diablo rises above the East Bay communities. Richardson Bay is directly below, along with Angel Island just beyond Tiburon and Belvedere.

To the northeast, College of Marin is nestled at the foot of the mountain. Just over the ridge from Kentfield is downtown San Rafael where Marin's beginnings are rooted at the Mission, established in 1817. To the north, the small lake is Lake Lagunitas and the larger one is Bon Tempe Lake.

Energetic members of your group can hike up the steep trail to the summit. The Gardner Fire Lookout, which stands atop East Peak, was built in 1937 and is not open to the public.

For hikers who want to walk to the summit, the Old Stage Road–Old Railroad Grade route is the most direct from Pantoll Ranger Station. This 7.5-mile round trip on well-graded fire roads features a stop at the historic West Point Inn and scenic views along the way.

In 1896 the Mt. Tamalpais and Muir Woods Railroad opened for business. It was highly publicized as the "Crookedest Railroad in the World," and it made Mt. Tamalpais world famous. In those days, no sightseeing trip to San Francisco was complete without a train ride to the top of Mt. Tam. The railroad was an amazing engineering feat. It traveled 8 miles up the mountain from Mill Valley to the summit through 281 curves. At the top was the Tavern of Tamalpais where visitors could wine, dine, and dance. The foundation of the Old Tavern is visible near today's summit parking area. The train declined in popularity after the first automobile road opened. Today, the old railroad grade is one of the most popular hiking trails on the mountain.

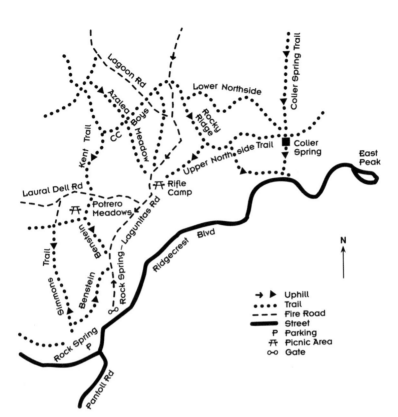

Potrero Meadows
Marin Municipal Water District

ACCESS: Ridgecrest Blvd. at Pantoll Road

POINTS OF INTEREST: Views, wildflowers, wildlife

DISTANCE: Simmons–Benstein Trails loop: 3 miles
Rock Spring–Lagunitas Road–Upper Northside–
Lower Northside–Rocky Ridge: 4 miles

DIFFICULTY: Moderate

INFORMATION: Marin Municipal Water District Ranger Office
(415) 945-1181

Potrero Meadows
Marin Municipal Water District

A massive landslide that occurred 2000 to 3000 years ago created the flat area known as Potrero Meadows. It was used as a campsite up until the 1960s. Today, there are picnic tables and restrooms at Potrero Meadows.

Located about 1 mile from the Rock Spring trailhead, the most direct routes to Potrero Meadows from Rock Spring are via the Benstein Trail, which is a footpath, or Rock Spring-Lagunitas Road.

The Simmons and the Benstein trails make a moderately difficult, 3-mile loop through a mixed forest of Douglas fir, madrone, tanoak and live oaks, and give hikers an opportunity to have lunch or a snack at Potrero Meadows. When walking this loop, start at the Rock Spring parking lot and watch for a wooden footbridge. Just after the bridge, the trail splits. Follow the Simmons Trail, which is the path that goes to the left up the hill. The trail that goes to the right alongside the creek is the Benstein. Pass Barth's Retreat and follow the Laurel Dell Fire Road to Potrero Meadows. The Benstein Trail is a forest path that joins the Rock Spring-Lagunitas Road for a distance of about 100 yards then branches off back into the woods.

From Potrero Meadows you can create an interesting 3-mile loop by walking the Rock Spring-Lagunitas Road to the Upper Northside Trail and turning left onto the Lower Northside Trail at the Colier Spring junction. Walk on the Rocky Ridge for a short distance before joining the Rock Spring-Lagunitas Road and follow it back to Rifle Camp and Rock Spring. This loop features extensive views to the north from the Upper and Lower Northside trails. Chaparral and manzanita line the brief walk on the Rocky Ridge.

For a challenging map-reading trek on forest trails, explore the Kent Trail, Azalea Meadow Trail, Lagoon Road, and Cross Country Boys Trail. Deep forest gives this area a real wilderness feeling, and though the trails are not difficult to walk, the challenge comes in reading the map and signs. This area is crisscrossed with trails, making it difficult at times to pinpoint your exact location. Despite a little confusion, you'll probably emerge at either Rifle Camp or Potrero Meadows. Rifle Camp is another picnic area that was a campsite. The name comes from an old rifle that was dug up by a dog.

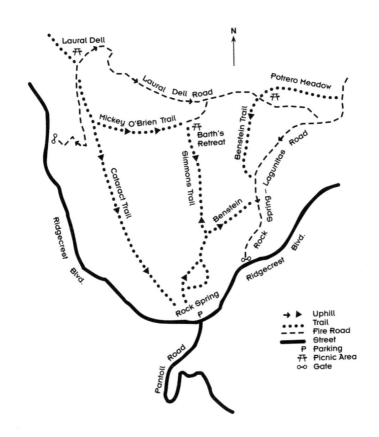

Uphill
Trail
Fire Road
Street
P Parking
⛾ Picnic Area
o∞ Gate

Rock Spring Trailhead
Marin Municipal Water District

ACCESS: Ridgecrest Blvd. at Pantoll Road

POINTS OF INTEREST: Waterfalls, wildflowers, views

DISTANCE: Cataract–Laural Dell–Rock Spring loop: 5 miles
Cataract–Mickey O'Brien–Simmons loop: 3.5 miles

DIFFICULTY: Moderate

INFORMATION: Marin Municipal Water District Ranger Office
(415) 945-1181

Rock Spring Trailhead
Marin Municipal Water District

Rock Spring is a popular trailhead with a large parking area. Several loop hikes can be created, and destinations all over Mt. Tamalpais can be reached from this starting point. The spring still seeps out of a large pile of rocks.

The Cataract Trail–Laurel Dell Road–Rock Spring-Lagunitas Road provides a good introductory loop with beautiful and varied scenery. The Cataract Trail is a footpath that parallels Cataract Creek as it winds through thick forest of redwood, bay, oak, and madrone. This area is a wildflower wonderland in the spring.

In 1945, a forest fire burned for seven days on the ridges above Cataract Creek. On the last day of that great fire, two Navy Corsair planes on maneuvers collided above Mt. Tam. Both pilots parachuted to safety, but the wreckage of one plane came crashing down near today's Cataract Trail, causing a fire that burned 200 more acres. Pieces of the plane are scattered on the hillside to the north of the trail. Part of an engine is in the creekbed and visible from the trail. During years of heavy rain fall, the engine has been pushed downstream. Some years, it's partially covered by debris and dirt, making it difficult to see.

The meadow at Laurel Dell is a picnic area today. It was a popular group campsite until the 1960s, when camping was prohibited on watershed lands. If you join the Laurel Dell Fire Road and follow it through open areas with chaparral, the road suddenly tops a hill, and magnificent views spread to the north, with Alpine Lake and the Meadow Club golf course below. Out on the horizon is Mt. Wittenberg on Point Reyes Peninsula and Tomales Bay. Fairfax, Big Rock Ridge, and Hamilton Field are also visible.

The large meadow at the Potrero picnic area was one of the first campsites on Mt. Tam. It was established as early as the 1850s and used until the 1960s. A massive landslide that occurred 2,000 to 3,000 years ago created the meadow.

The Rock Spring-Lagunitas Road connects Lake Lagunitas and Rock Spring. As you proceed along Laural Dell Road, continue through Potrero Meadows, turn right onto the Rock Spring-Lagunitas Road and follow it to Rock Spring parking area.

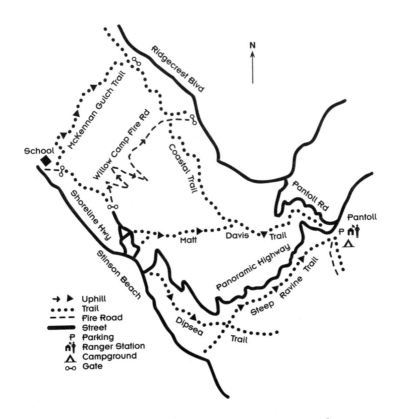

Willow Camp Fire Road
Mt. Tamalpais State Park

ACCESS: Shoreline Highway or Ridgecrest Blvd.

POINTS OF INTEREST: Views, wildflowers, wildlife

DISTANCE: Willow Camp–Coastal–Matt Davis loop: 5 miles
Stinson Beach to Pantoll via Matt Davis: 3.5 miles
Stinson Beach to Pantoll via Steep Ravine: 3 miles

DIFFICULTY: Moderate/Strenuous

INFORMATION: Mt. Tamalpais State Park
(415) 388-2070

Willow Camp Fire Road
Mt. Tamalpais State Park

The west side of Mt. Tamalpais, above Stinson Beach, offers trails with magnificent views of Bolinas Lagoon, Stinson Beach, the Golden Gate, and the Pacific Ocean out to the Farallon Islands. This side of Mt. Tam is the most exposed to weather. Summer fog can encase it in cool moisture, blustery winter winds can sweep it relentlessly, while on clear sunny days the temperature can be anywhere from pleasant to unbearably hot. When hiking these trails, take extra care in preparation: wear layered clothes and always carry a windbreaker and plenty of water.

The Willow Camp Fire Road got its name from the small community of Willow Camp, which today is known as Stinson Beach. Except for a section shaded by huge old Douglas firs near the top, this trail zigzags through open grassland. The views are breathtaking.

The Coastal Trail is nearly level along the contour of the Mountain. Ridgecrest Boulevard was built in 1925 and operated as a toll road until 1942, when the Army took over the top of Mt. Tamalpais and closed the road to civilian traffic. In 1945, the road was reopened, and in 1948 it became part of Mt. Tamalpais State Park.

The McKennan Gulch Trail climbs 1,600 feet in elevation from Shoreline Highway right next to the Bolinas-Stinson Beach School to Ridgecrest Boulevard. There are many wide-open views along this trail. Near the top is where prospectors hunted for copper in the 1930s. The McKennan–Coastal–Willow Camp Fire Road can be walked as a loop.

The Steep Ravine Trail lives up to its name. It's a steep trail that winds beside Webb Creek and its many small waterfalls. At one point hikers must climb a ladder to continue on the trail. This hike is a real adventure through a botanical wonderland during the spring and summer.

The Matt Davis Trail offers a less strenuous route than the Dipsea–Steep Ravine trails from Stinson Beach to Pantoll Ranger Station. It begins with zigzags through a Douglas fir forest near Stinson Beach and travels via gently graded trail across open grassland to Pantoll. Spring wildflowers are lovely along this path.

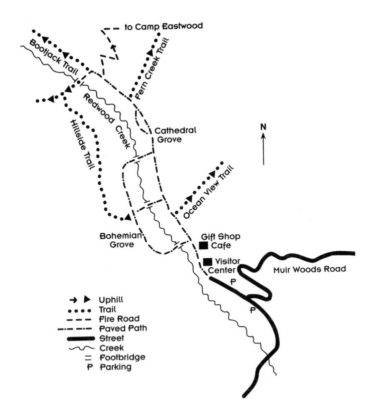

to Camp Eastwood

Bootjack Trail

Fern Creek Trail

Redwood Creek

Hillside Trail

Cathedral Grove

N

Ocean View Trail

Bohemian Grove

Gift Shop
Cafe

Visitor Center

Muir Woods Road

P

P

→ ▶ Uphill
•••• Trail
– – – Fire Road
–··–··– Paved Path
━━━ Street
〜〜 Creek
= Footbridge
P Parking

Muir Woods
Muir Woods National Monument

ACCESS: Muir Woods Road off Panoramic Highway

POINTS OF INTEREST: Giant redwood trees, wildflowers

DISTANCE: Muir Woods loop: 2 miles
Fern Creek–Camp Eastwood loop: 1.5 miles

DIFFICULTY: Easy

INFORMATION: Muir Woods National Monument
(415) 388-2595

Muir Woods
Muir Woods National Monument

The main path through the heart of Muir Woods National Monument is an easy 1-mile walk on a paved path which is wheelchair and stroller accessible. There are also many benches along the way. A visitor's center, a gift shop, a cafe, and restrooms are available.

Redwood trees are famous for their height and straight grain. In Muir Woods, many of the redwoods are over 240 feet tall and approximately 500–800 years old. They gain enormous girth because conditions at this location are nearly perfect. Moisture is provided by rain in the winter and fog in the summer. The depth of the ravine protects the trees from wind and sun. While the growing conditions are perfect for redwood trees, the lack of sunlight reaching the forest floor makes living conditions difficult for other trees and plants. Bay trees lean so far attempting to reach sunlight that they fall and uproot themselves.

The four bridges across Redwood Creek are excellent viewpoints for watching fish in winter. December through March is spawning time for the steelhead trout and coho salmon, which fight their way up the creek to lay their eggs.

Redwood trees are fire resistant. This is due to the tannic acid that flows within the tree and the thick layers of fibrous bark. You will see trees with fire scars. A redwood can continue to grow even with half its base hollowed by fire.

You can extend your walk and increase views of the magnificent redwoods by exploring the Fern Creek Trail (to Camp Eastwood) or hiking along the Hillside Trail. Dress warmly for your visit—the Woods are cold and damp even on sunny days.

In 1908, Muir Woods was declared a National Monument by President Theodore Roosevelt. The land had been donated to the federal government by William Kent to protect it from logging and a threat to dam the canyon. Kent requested that the woods be named for the famous conservationist, John Muir.

Please note that picnicking is not allowed in Muir Woods. You can enjoy your lunch at vacant tables in Camp Eastwood or at nearby Muir Beach. The entrance fee to Muir Woods National Monument is $2 for visitors over age 17.

Fern Creek Trail
Muir Woods National Monument

ACCESS: Panoramic Highway or Muir Woods Road

POINTS OF INTEREST: Giant redwood trees, wildflowers

DISTANCE: Panoramic–Ocean View–Muir Woods–
 Fern Creek–Camp Eastwood loop: 5 miles

DIFFICULTY: Moderate

INFORMATION: Muir Woods National Monument
 (415) 388-2595

Fern Creek Trail
Muir Woods National Monument

The ridges surrounding Muir Woods provide excellent hiking trails that showcase the giant redwoods. The Panoramic Trail, Ocean View Trail, Muir Woods path, Fern Creek Trail, and Camp Eastwood Road combine to create a moderately strenuous, 5-mile loop with a 700-foot climb in elevation.

Begin the loop at the parking area opposite the Mountain Home Inn on Panoramic Highway. Follow the Panoramic Trail as it weaves through oak woodland, then descend the Ocean View Trail into dense redwood forest with Douglas fir and California nutmeg.

At the junction with the main trail in Muir Woods National Monument, turn right and walk along Redwood Creek for most of a mile. Enjoy Cathedral Grove, which encompasses some of the tallest and oldest trees in Muir Woods. The Fern Creek Trail junction is a quarter-mile past Cathedral Grove. Fern Creek's rushing water tumbles over boulders and downed trees as it hurries to join Redwood Creek. The setting looks like a tropical paradise with lush ferns and waterfalls spilling into emerald pools. Spring wildflowers include trillium, forget-me-nots, and fairy lanterns. Horsetails poke up alongside the creek.

Near the junction of the Lost Trail is a long, sloping footbridge. The dog-leg angle at the end of the bridge gives it unique design. Cross the footbridge and continue on the Fern Creek Trail to Camp Eastwood, which is located within the boundaries of Mt. Tamalpais State Park. This group campsite provides restrooms and picnic tables, making it a good spot for lunch or a snack. Remember that picnicking is not allowed in Muir Woods National Monument.

Complete the loop hike by walking up Camp Eastwood Road. Tall redwoods and Douglas firs create a nearly solid canopy overhead, making this a cool hike even on a warm summer day. Characteristics of the forest change as you rise in elevation. Oak trees replace redwoods at the crest of the ridge. After finishing the loop hike, you may want to cross Panoramic Highway and make a brief visit to the Mountain Home Inn where you can enjoy the view of Mill Valley, Blithedale Ridge, Ring Mountain, and San Francisco.

The entrance fee to Muir Woods is $2 for visitors over age 17.

Legend:
- → ▶ Uphill
- •••• Trail
- – – Fire Road
- –••– Paved Path
- ▬ Street
- P Parking
- ♟♦ Ranger Station
- ⅂ Picnic Area
- △ Campground
- o–o Gate

Ben Johnson Trail
Mt. Tamalpais State Park

ACCESS: Muir Woods Road off Panoramic Highway

POINTS OF INTEREST: Giant redwood trees, wildflowers

DISTANCE: Camp Eastwood–Ben Johnson–Stapelveldt–TCC–
   Troop 80 loop: 7 miles
   Bootjack–TCC–Stapelveldt–Ben Johnson loop: 5 miles

DIFFICULTY: Moderate/Strenuous

INFORMATION: Mt. Tamalpais State Park
   (415) 388-2070

Ben Johnson Trail
Mt. Tamalpais State Park

Mt. Tamalpais State Park completely encircles Muir Woods National Monument. A trek through the magnificent giant redwoods is an added bonus to any Mt. Tam hike. When planning your hike, remember that picnicking is not allowed in Muir Woods.

For a strenuous 7-mile loop, combine the Camp Eastwood Road, Ben Johnson Trail, Stapelveldt Trail, TCC Trail, and Troop 80 Trail. Beginning at the parking area near Mountain Home Inn, walk down the road to Camp Eastwood. A group camp is located on the site of one of the old inns that graced the area around Muir Woods in the early 1900s. It is named for Alice Eastwood, a chief botanist for the California Academy of Science. During the 1906 earthquake and fire, this courageous woman personally saved many valuable botanical records. Ironically, during the Big Fire of 1929 that raged up Mt. Tam, Alice Eastwood was one of about 100 Mill Valley residents to lose her home.

Skirt the end of Muir Woods, join the Ben Johnson Trail and continue up on the Stapelveldt. These paths head up steadily all the way up to the TCC Trail weaving alongside a scenic, deep ravine, shaded by thick redwood forest. The TCC Trail's level course snakes along the contour of the mountain. Huge Douglas fir dominate this part of the forest, and huckleberry bushes grow so tall along some sections of this path that they create a tunnel of vegetation.

Van Wyck Meadow is a small clearing that makes a nice spot for a snack or lunch. The last two miles along the Troop 80 Trail reveal a variety of landscape.

For a shorter version of this hike, try the 5-mile loop created by the Bootjack–TCC–Stapelveldt–Ben Johnson trails. The Bootjack Trail between Muir Woods and Bootjack Picnic Area is a steep climb that rises 1,000 feet in 2 miles. It follows the upper reaches of Redwood Creek, which snakes and tumbles through a deep ravine with moss-covered boulders, ferns, and a variety of native trees. Beautiful cascades, waterfalls, and wildflowers make every step of the steep climb worth the effort. Spectacular during the winter and spring runoff, the stream's steady flow often lasts well into summer, making this a lovely warm-weather hike as well.

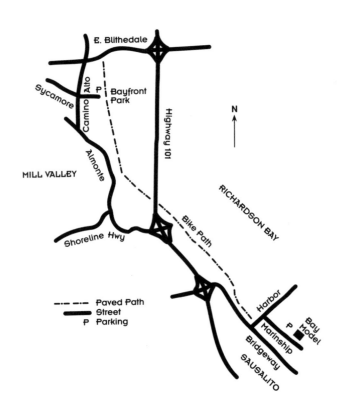

Bothin Marsh
Marin Open Space District

ACCESS: Bayfront Park, Sycamore Avenue

POINTS OF INTEREST: Paved level path, waterfowl

DISTANCE: Marsh walk (one way): 1.5 miles

DIFFICULTY: Easy

INFORMATION: Marin County Open Space
(415) 499-6405

Bothin Marsh
Marin Open Space District

The large marsh area bordering Richardson Bay is Bothin Marsh, owned by the Marin County Open Space District. This marsh is a saltwater sanctuary. At low tide the mud flats are exposed, providing excellent feeding opportunities for birds. You'll probably see hundreds of shorebirds wading and huge gatherings of gulls. A pair of binoculars will help you identify ducks, egrets, and herons.

Today's paved path is located on the old railroad levee. From the 1880s through the 1930s trains were a very important part of Marin's transportation system. This railroad line connected with a ferry at the tip of Sausalito. At "The Hub" in San Anselmo, the tracks joined with the San Rafael line. A train known as *The Special* transported students from San Anselmo, Ross, Kentfield, and Corte Madera to Tamalpais High School

You can extend your walk or bike ride with a visit to the Bay Model by turning left on Harbor Street and following the signs a third of a mile. The San Francisco Bay and Delta Model Visitor Center is open to the public, free of charge. The huge facility is maintained by the U.S. Army Corps of Engineers. Many studies and tests on the rise and fall of tides, water currents, mixing of salt and fresh water, and sediment movements are done here. For more information about the Bay Model, call (415) 332-3871.

Across the highway at the eastern end of the path is Marin City. This area sprang to life during World War II as a housing facility for the thousands of workers at the nearby Marinship shipyard on the Sausalito waterfront. Between 1942 and 1945, Marinship built and launched 93 ships.

In 1822, a young British sailor, William Richardson, arrived in California. He applied for Mexican citizenship so that he could remain as a permanent resident. To qualify for Mexican citizenship, he had to become a Catholic and take a Mexican name. In 1838, Captain William Antonio Richardson was granted 20,000 acres of hilly land that extended from Sausalito to Mill Valley and out to the Pacific Ocean. The land grant was named Rancho Sausalito, meaning "place of the small willows" for the willow trees that grew near the hillside springs.

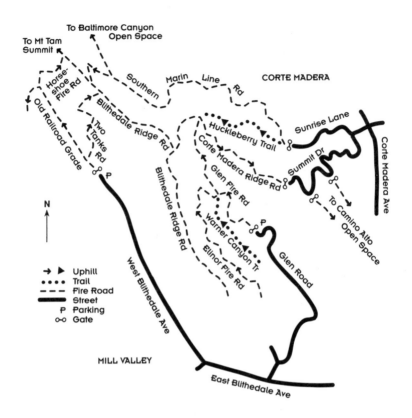

Blithedale Ridge
Marin Open Space District

ACCESS: Summit Drive, Glen Road, West Blithedale

POINTS OF INTEREST: Views, wildflowers, wildlife

DISTANCE: Two Tanks–Blithedale Ridge–Corte Madera–
             Huckleberry- Southern Marin Line: 4 miles

DIFFICULTY: Moderate

INFORMATION: Marin County Open Space
                (415) 499-6405

Blithedale Ridge
Marin Open Space District

Blithedale and Corte Madera ridges offer excellent hiking, biking, and horseback-riding trails. The fire protection road system on these ridges is extensive and can be connected with Baltimore Canyon Open Space, Camino Alto Open Space, and the Marin Municipal Water District lands for routes to the reservoirs or the summit of Mt. Tamalpais.

The fire roads on Blithedale Ridge are well graded and have only a few steep sections. Some of the mid-ridge fire roads are nearly level, curving along the contours of the hills. The routes from West Blithdale wind up the ridge, climbing 300 feet.

Huckleberry Trail is a footpath that connects the level Southern Marin Line Road with the Corte Madera Ridge Road. It is a typical mountain trail, winding through its namesake, huckleberry bushes. This trail journeys in and out of chaparral thick with manzanita, shady redwood groves with ferns, and woodland of live oak, bay, and madrone. This well-traveled path climbs steadily, but the climb is hardly noticeable with so much variety of plants to examine along the way.

Views from the ridge-top fire roads stretch to the horizon. San Francisco Bay looms large, with the towns of Mill Valley, Sausalito, Corte Madera, and Larkspur tucked around its edges. Mt. Tamalpais rises 2,572 feet, filling the western sky. The fire lookout on its summit is clearly visible and appears deceptively close. When you stand on the crest of either Corte Madera Ridge or Blithedale Ridge, you are at approximately 900 feet in elevation, or approximately one third of the way to Mt. Tam's summit.

The vegetation along the ridge varies depending on the amount of sunlight and moisture. Crowded into ravines are moisture-loving trees and plants. You'll see buckeye trees, redwoods, and an occasional Douglas fir. In the drier areas, live oaks thrive in addition to coyote bush and chamise.

The name Blithedale comes from a sanitarium that was built deep in the Mill Valley canyon in 1870. By 1880, the sanitarium was converted into a resort hotel and the name generalized into an area name, including Blithedale Canyon and Blithedale Ridge.

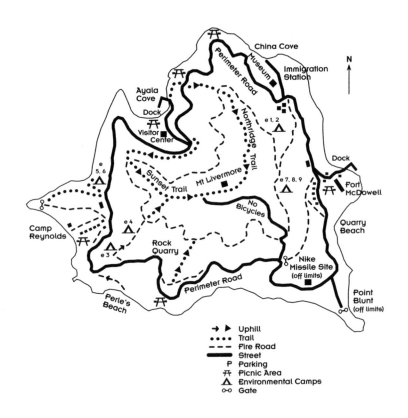

Angel Island Summit
Angel Island State Park

ACCESS: Ferry to Ayala Cove

POINTS OF INTEREST: Views, historical buildings, wildflowers

DISTANCE: Sunset–Northridge loop: 2 miles

DIFFICULTY: Moderate

INFORMATION: Angel Island State Park (415) 435-1915
                  Tiburon Ferry (415) 435-2131
                  Blue & Gold Fleet (415) 773-1188
                  Alameda/Oakland Ferry (415) 705-5555

Angel Island Summit
Angel Island State Park

At slightly more than a square mile in size, Angel Island State Park is the largest island in San Francisco Bay. The hike up to Mt. Livermore's summit features forested ridges, grass hillsides, spring wildflowers, and a 360-degree view.

Follow the Sunset Trail to the 781-foot summit of Mt. Livermore. Only a short distance up the trail is a fine view of Raccoon Strait. This 1-mile wide channel between Angel Island and Tiburon got its name from the HMS *Raccoon*, a 16-gun sloop-of-war that spent two months on the beach at Ayala Cove for repairs in 1814.

Continue up the main ridge through grassland and forest. The anti-aircraft guns, searchlight, and Nike Missile Control that were once located on the mountaintop are now gone. Today, picnic tables mark the summit. The view from this point is spectacular with a unique perspective of the surrounding bay and communities. The Northridge Trail continues the loop back down to Ayala Cove. Watch for hawks overhead, song birds in the bushes, deer grazing on the grass hillsides, and wildflowers displaying a rainbow of colors in the spring and early summer.

Historically, Angel Island has always been a significant place. Indians paddled their tule boats over to village sites that date back at least 3,000 years. In the late 1700s, the ships of explorers, whalers, and even pirates stopped at the island to gather firewood. Russian sea otter hunters had a camp here in the early 1800s. Then a Mexican land grant gave the island to Don Antonio Maria Osio, who grazed cattle on it. In 1850, the U.S. Government obtained possession of the property. The first gun batteries and structures appeared in 1863 during the Civil War. The military occupation of Angel Island lasted 100 years, ending in 1964 when the Nike Missile Site was deactivated.

Ayala Cove, where the ferry from Tiburon docks, was where the Spanish mariner Juan Manual de Ayala anchored his ship in 1775. Lt. Ayala gave Angel Island its name. The name Ayala Cove, however, was not assigned until the Cove's renaming in 1969, a full 194 years after his visit. Before that, it was Hospital Cove and the site of the Quarantine Station from 1892 to 1952.

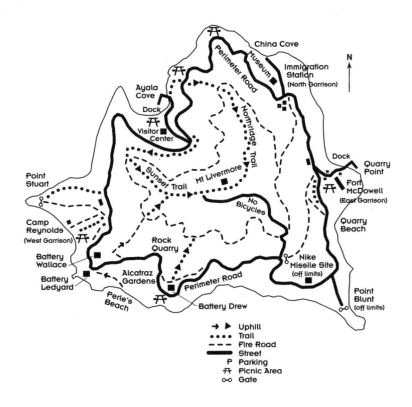

Angel Island Loop
Angel Island State Park

ACCESS: Ferry to Ayala Cove

POINTS OF INTEREST: Views, historical buildings, museum

DISTANCE: Island loop on Perimeter Road: 5 miles

DIFFICULTY: Easy

INFORMATION: Angel Island State Park (415) 435-1915
Tiburon Ferry (415) 435-2131
Blue & Gold Fleet (415) 773-1188
Alameda/Oakland Ferry (415) 705-5555

Angel Island Loop
Angel Island State Park

The Perimeter Road provides an easy 5-mile loop that introduces visitors to the island's history. In wartime, Angel Island was one of the busiest military posts in the United States.

Heading south on the Perimeter Road after leaving Ayala Cove brings you to Camp Reynolds (West Garrison), the first military fortification on the Island. It served as the living quarters for the men in the artillery units. Surviving buildings include the bakery, blacksmith shop, chapel, stables, and the storehouse near the water.

Continuing on the Perimeter Road, you come to Fort McDowell (East Garrison). This ghost town of huge buildings stands as a sober reminder of the hundreds of thousands of soldiers that were sent off to war or returned from war to this depot. It began as a detention camp in 1898 for troops returning from the Spanish-American War and the Philippines. By 1911, Fort McDowell had evolved into a large military induction center. It received recruits, trained them, and processed them for overseas assignment. An average of 30,000 men a year passed through this facility. Buildings still remaining are the 800-man barracks; the mess hall that could seat 1,410 men at a time; the guard house that held 60 prisoners; the post exchange with a store, coffee shop, and offices; a 70-bed hospital that stands at the end of the officer's row of houses. This hospital building was later used as headquarters for the Nike Missle Command.

Rounding the north end of the island, you come to the Immigration Station (North Garrison). The Immigration Detention Center operated from 1910 to 1940. During those years, 175,000 immigrants, most of them Chinese, passed through this center. The average stay was two weeks to six months. When the large administration building burned in 1940, it marked the end of the detention center at this location. The museum is open March through October, on Saturdays, Sundays, and holidays.

China Cove has a small beach facing north. It is a peaceful and scenic spot today, in contrast to the difficult time immigrants endured here at the Immigration Detention Center, or the discouraging days the World War II prisoners-of-war must have experienced while incarcerated here.

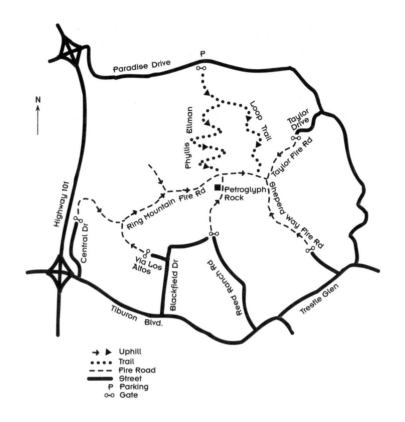

Ring Mountain Preserve
Marin Open Space District

ACCESS: Paradise Drive, 1.5 miles from Highway 101

POINTS OF INTEREST: Views, rare wildflowers, petroglyphs

DISTANCE: Phyllis Ellman–Loop Trail: 2.5 miles

DIFFICULTY: Moderate

INFORMATION: Marin County Open Space
(415) 499-6405

Ring Mountain Preserve
Marin Open Space District

Ring Mountain is the ridge that separates Corte Madera and Tiburon. It offers excellent hiking trails, historical sights, rare wildflowers, and scenic views.

The Phyllis Ellman Trail and the Loop Trail combine to make a 2.5-mile circle of the preserve. Begin at the Phyllis Ellman Trail on Paradise Drive in Corte Madera. Turn left and follow the Loop Trail (also signed Nature Trail) as it winds up to the top of the 600-foot summit. Seasonal interpretive brochures are available that discuss wildflowers, geological features, and animal habitat at numbered posts along the way.

In prehistoric times, Indians occupied the area. Take the short spur trail left to the streambed to see a depression in the stone that may have been used for grinding acorn flour.

Farther up the Loop Trail near the ridge top, the path passes through clumps of old trees that provide a shaded lunch nook, but watch out for poison oak.

At the junction with the Ring Mountain Fire Road, turn right and walk downhill to the saddle in the ridge. Take a short detour to the left to see the boulder with Petroglyphs on it. The curiously carved circular symbols could be as old as 2,000 years, and their meaning is still a mystery.

From the crest of the ridge, views extend to San Francisco, Tiburon, Belvedere, Sausalito, Mill Valley, and all the way around to Mt. Tamalpais, Corte Madera, Larkspur, San Quentin, and Richmond. When you're ready, head down the Phyllis Ellman Trail.

Geologically speaking, the footpaths cross an ancient landslide. The green serpentine is an unusual mineral that has created unique growing conditions for plants. As a result, Ring Mountain is home to seven rare species of plants, including the Tiburon mariposa lily, which grows nowhere else in the world.

Ring Mountain is named for the dairyman George E. Ring who owned land near Paradise Cay from 1879 to 1911. In 1950, four 90mm anti-aircraft guns and other military structures were placed on the east knoll of the ridge. Today, the military installation is gone, with only the level area and service road visible.

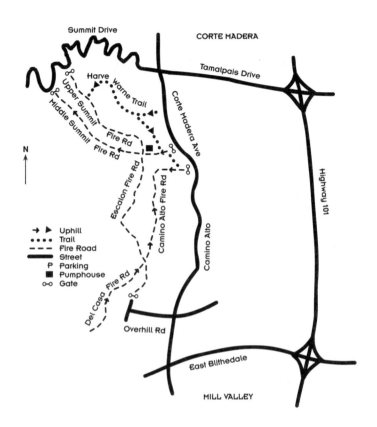

Camino Alto
Marin Open Space District

ACCESS: Corte Madera Avenue, Camino Alto, Overhill Road

POINTS OF INTEREST: Views, wildflowers, wildlife

DISTANCE: Upper Summit–Middle Summit–Escalon–Camino
Alto: 3.5 miles, strenuous
Escalon–Camino Alto: 1.5 miles, easy

DIFFICULTY: Easy, Strenuous

INFORMATION: Marin County Open Space
(415) 499-6405

Camino Alto
Marin Open Space District

The Camino Alto Open Space, on the ridge between Corte Madera and Mill Valley, offers a variety of trails from level walking to strenuous climbing.

The main access is on Corte Madera Avenue at the gate with the green open-space sign. The trail is steep for a short distance to the intersection of fire roads with a small pump house. At the intersection you can choose whatever type of hike suits your skill.

For a strenuous 3.5-mile outing, combine all four fireroads, Upper Summit, Middle Summit, Escalon, and Camino Alto into a figure eight by using a short walk on Summit Drive to connect the trails. Summit Drive is narrow and very steep with some traffic, so use caution while walking on it. Sweeping views from the ridge top include Mill Valley's fingerlike ravines, Richardson Bay, and San Francisco Bay.

For a 1.5-mile, mildly strenuous loop, explore Escalon Fire Road and the Camino Alto Fire Road. Blithedale Ridge, Tiburon, Belvedere, Angel Island, and parts of Mill Valley are visible from viewpoints along the way.

If easy suits you, enjoy a 2.5-mile out-and-back saunter on the nearly level Escalon and Upper Summit fire roads. These smooth roads wind through mix oak forest on the south-facing slope and groves of redwoods on the cool, shady north-facing side. You may notice that the redwood trees are uniform in size. The Corte Madera and Larkspur hillsides below the Upper Summit Fire Road were logged in the 1860s. What you see today is a second-growth forest, now over 140 years old.

For an interesting loop on a footpath, include the Harve Warne Trail in your hike. This path weaves through a thick forest with lush ferns as it parellels Corte Madera Avenue.

This land was part of John Reed's Corte Madera del Presidio land grant in 1834. Reed's sawmill was located on Cascade Creek in Mill Valley. After an intense period of logging from 1850 to 1880, the forests were gone and dairy ranching became prominent. "Alto" means "high" in Spanish. By 1874 when the railroad tracks reached the top of Corte Madera Ridge, Alto Pass was an established name.

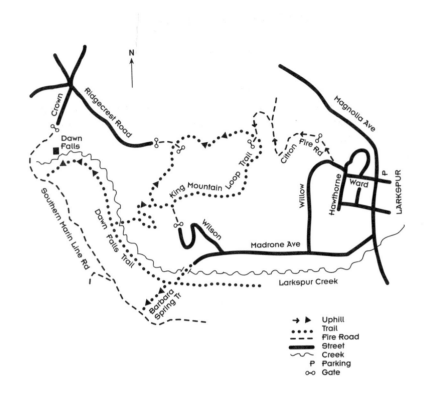

Baltimore Canyon
Marin Open Space District

ACCESS: Madrone Avenue, Wilson Way, Crown Road

POINTS OF INTEREST: Creek walk, old dam, waterfall

DISTANCE: Dawn Falls Trail: 1 mile
King Mountain Loop: 2 miles

DIFFICULTY: Moderate

INFORMATION: Marin County Open Space
(415) 499-6405

Baltimore Canyon
Marin Open Space District

A hike into Baltimore Canyon along Larkspur Creek is not only a lovely nature walk, but also a journey back into history. The steep canyon walls of today are covered with redwood trees, ferns, moss-covered bay trees, shrubs, and countless delicate wildflowers. Take time to investigate the old stumps left from the logging days.

The 1-mile trail to Dawn Falls is level for more than half the distance before turning sharply uphill for the final climb to the falls. The narrow footpath winds alongside the creek. The steep climb to the falls is rewarded with views of water pouring over a rocky lip and frothing white as it splashes into the pool below.

To create a loop hike, continue up the trail above the falls. Turn left on the Southern Marin Line Road and walk along the contour of the ridge. After about one mile, watch for a signpost on the left marking the Barbara Spring Trail. Hiking down the Barbara Spring Trail returns you to the Dawn Falls Trail near the footbridge.

In 1850, a sawmill was built at the mouth of the canyon by the Baltimore & Frederick Mining & Trading Company of Baltimore, Maryland. Large sawed-off stumps and the uniform size of the second growth redwoods serve as a reminder that this area was totally denuded in the ten years the sawmill was in operation. The lumber was shipped across the bay and used to build the San Francisco Presidio. In 1881, just when the new young trees had started to cover the hillsides, a fire started in Baltimore Canyon and swept up Mt. Tamalpais. It burned for one week and destroyed 50,000 acres.

Two natural springs flow out of the ridge and over Dawn Falls. These springs were a source of water for the young town of Larkspur. The old rock dam is still visible today. It was built by the Larkspur Water Company sometime between 1888 and 1903 of locally quarried blue basalt.

King Mountain Open Space Preserve may also be accessed from Baltimore Canyon. About halfway to the waterfall, a trail splits off, to the right, crosses the creek, and heads up the hillside. It joins the King Mountain Loop Trail (Public Trail), a 2-mile footpath that circles the top of King Mountain above Larkspur. This hike features redwood and mixed forest, spring wildflowers, and scenic views.

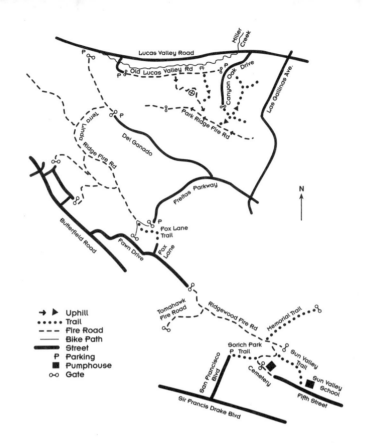

Terra Linda/Sleepy Hollow Divide
Marin Open Space District

ACCESS: Lucas Valley Road, Canyon Oak Drive, Del Ganado Road, Freitas Parkway, San Francisco Blvd.

POINTS OF INTEREST: Views, wildflowers, wildlife

DISTANCE: Old Lucas Valley Road: 1 mile, easy
　　　　　　Terra Linda Ridge Fire Road: 2 miles, moderate
　　　　　　Ridgewood Fire Road: 1 mile, easy

DIFFICULTY: Easy, Moderate

INFORMATION: Marin County Open Space
　　　　　　　(415) 499-6405

Terra Linda/Sleepy Hollow Divide
Marin Open Space District

The Terra Linda/Sleepy Hollow Divide Open Space Preserve nearly encircles the community of Terra Linda. There is a mildly strenuous walk of about 1.5 miles from Lucas Valley Road to the Park Ridge Fire Road, and the ridge top exploration is highlighted with sweeping views. Beginning at the west end of Old Lucas Valley Road, walk along the old pavement that parallels Miller Creek. Head up the fire road that winds past a water tank and continues to the top of the ridge. As you wander along the fire road on the crest of the ridge, you'll have an unobstructed view to the south.

Hiking along the ridge that separates Terra Linda and Sleepy Hollow provides a moderately strenuous, 2-mile walk on the Terra Linda Ridge Fire Road. Beginning at the end of Del Ganado Road in Terra Linda, walk up the trail about 300 yards to the junction of fire roads. Turn left and continue up the ridge. The steep climb in elevation provides an excellent view of the Terra Linda valley framed by the forested San Pedro Ridge in the distance. The fire road merges with an old paved driveway. Follow the driveway to the junction with the paved bike path. Turn left and follow the bike path down to the end of Manuel T. Freitas Parkway in Terra Linda.

Fire roads and trails on the San Rafael Ridge separating San Anselmo and Terra Linda offer views extending to San Francisco Bay. With access from both sides, the trails along the 1-mile-long summit are popular for walking, jogging, dog walking, and bike riding. From the end of Manuel T. Freitas Parkway in Terra Linda, walk up the paved bike path to the top of the small saddle and turn left onto the Fox Lane Trail, a footpath marked with a green trail sign. This trail meanders through a forest of oak, bay, and buckeye trees to Fox Lane. Walk along the street and turn left onto Fawn Drive. Proceed to the end of Fawn Drive's pavement and join the Ridgewood Fire Road on the top of San Rafael Ridge.

The access from San Anselmo is through Sorich Ranch Park, which provides a parking area. The trail weaves through a grove of tall eucalyptus trees as it zigzags toward the ridge top. Unlike the treeless western end of the ridge, the eastern end is shaded by old eucalyptus trees.

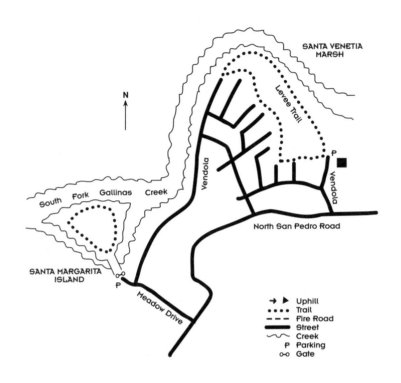

Santa Venetia Marsh
Marin Open Space District

ACCESS: End of Vendola Drive, end of Meadow Drive, and
other streets

POINTS OF INTEREST: Island, marsh, waterfowl

DISTANCE: Levee Trail: 1 mile
Santa Margarita Island loop: .8 mile

DIFFICULTY: Easy

INFORMATION: Marin County Open Space
(415) 499-6405

Santa Venetia Marsh
Marin Open Space District

The Santa Venetia Marsh Levee Trail gives good views of both the marsh area and the tidal zone of Gallinas Creek. This low-lying neighborhood is protected from tidal waters by a series of levees. The levees are ideal for viewing waterfowl. Binoculars and a bird identification book are handy on this walk.

Egrets are easy to locate because of their white plumage against the green cord grass and pickleweed or dark mud. They are seen standing motionless or wading in shallow water searching for insects and small fish. The great blue heron also frequents saltwater marshes, but its blue-gray coloring makes it more difficult to see. In winter, watch for the pintail duck with its long, slender, pointed tail. The shoveler is named for its spoon-shaped bill. Ruddy ducks have a distinctive short, stiff tail that points straight up.

Santa Margarita Island is an interesting little island with a level walking trail around it. A tree-covered hill in the center of the island provides a nice shady spot. It is also a good place to have a lesson on poison oak. "Leaves of three, let it be" will help you to watch for the characteristic three leaflets. An assortment of wildflowers bloom on the island during the spring and summer.

The bridge that connects the island is a good place to see mallards that patrol the surrounding waters. Mallards are Marin's most common duck. Mallard ducklings are born in the spring and summer. Eggs in a single clutch hatch within a few hours. As soon as the ducklings are dry after hatching, the mother leads them to water, where they are able to swim and feed themselves. The mother will teach the youngsters and protect them until they are able to fly, 49 to 60 days, at which time they are independent.

The cement chunks visible on the mud near the bridge to Santa Margarita Island are the remains of a levee built by the developer Mabry McMahan. In 1914, McMahan planned an elaborate Venetian-style creekside neighborhood that would have included gondolas imported from Venice to float up and down the South Fork of Las Gallinas Creek. However, World War I interrupted the plans. The name of the community and street names still reflect the original ideas and honor Mabry McMahan.

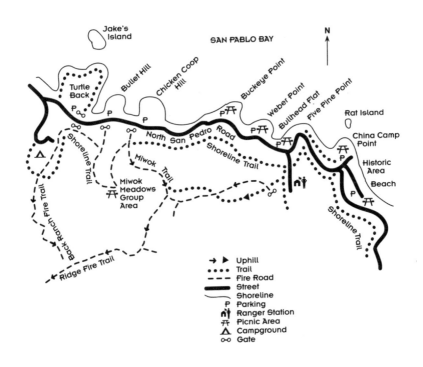

China Camp Shoreline
China Camp State Park

ACCESS: North San Pedro Road

POINTS OF INTEREST: Waterfowl, wildflowers, views

DISTANCE: Shoreline Trail (one way): 4 miles
Turtle Back Nature Trail: .5 mile

DIFFICULTY: Easy

INFORMATION: China Camp State Park
(415) 456-0766

China Camp Shoreline
China Camp State Park

From China Camp Point, above the historic village, you can observe Rat Island just off shore. A trail from the picnic area winds down to a small beach at Rat Rock Cove. The trail continues to Five Pine Point, which is a good fishing spot when the tide is high and an excellent bird-watching location when the tide is low.

The Shoreline Trail is an easy, 4-mile trail. It begins at the campground and parallels North San Pedro Road to the historic Chinese fishing village and beach. The route curves in and out of oak woodlands and features scenic bay views. Since the Shoreline Trail is long, you can walk as far as you want then return via the same path. On a warm day, the 2-mile section between Miwok Meadows and Bullhead Flat is shady and cool.

Scenic views to the north across San Pablo Bay are featured at the picnic areas on Weber Point and Buckeye Point. Picnic tables and parking are available at these locations. You may notice remains of old homesites. China Camp became a State Park in 1977; up until then, many parcels along the shoreline were privately owned.

The bluff at Buckeye Point provides a good vantage point for bird-watching. The surrounding mudflats attract numerous egrets, herons, willets, marbled godwits, and sand pipers at low tide.

The four hills, Chicken Coop Hill, Bullet Hill, Turtle Back, and Jake's Island were all islands in the days when the bay waters were deeper. Today, the little knobs still resemble islands. Turtle Back has a .5-mile nature trail that circles it.

Many animals, including raccoons, opossums, rabbits, skunks, squirrels, weasels, and mice live on the former islands. Larger mammals such as fox, bobcat, and deer come down from the nearby ridge to hunt and forage, so watch for their signs along the trails.

The marshes along China Camp's shoreline are an important habitat for many shore birds and ducks. They are also the home of two rare and endangered species: the tiny San Francisco Bay Saltmarsh Harvest Mouse and the Clapper Rail. The Clapper Rail is a duck-sized bird characterized by a stuffy, up-cocked tail, a short neck and a long bill with a slight downward curve. This bird prefers walking and will only take flight when absolutely necessary.

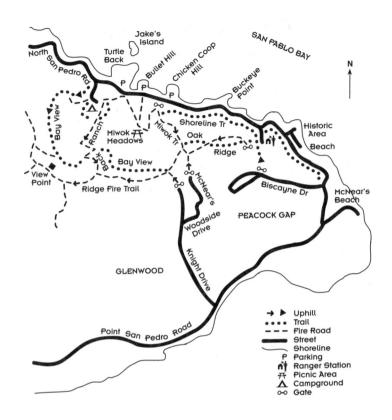

China Camp Ridge
China Camp State Park

ACCESS: North San Pedro Road

POINTS OF INTEREST: Waterfowl, wildflowers, views

DISTANCE: Back Ranch–Ridge–Miwok: 4 miles, strenuous
Bayview–Miwok–Shoreline: 6 miles, moderate

DIFFICULTY: Moderate, Strenuous

INFORMATION: China Camp State Park
(415) 456-0766

China Camp Ridge
China Camp State Park

The Back Ranch Meadow is the former site of the McNear family ranch. For many years the McNear cattle roamed the hills and meadows that are now China Camp State Park. In 1868, John and George McNear purchased this land. The McNear family home was located on the other side of the ridge in what is now the Glenwood neighborhood. To them the Ranch seemed "way back in the hills" and thus became known as Back Ranch. Today, a walk-in campground is located in the Back Ranch Meadow.

The 4-mile loop created by the Back Ranch Fire Trail–Ridge Fire Trail–Miwok Trail is strenuous, with several steep sections. Literally starting at sea level, you'll climb 1,000-feet in elevation to reach the crest of the ridge. The Back Ranch Fire Trail begins behind the campground and zigzags up the ridge through a mixed forest of live oak, bay, and madrone. To reach the ridge's summit, turn right and go uphill on the Ridge Fire Trail. Continue for a half mile to the old Nike site. The Nike Missile radar tracking station that was here during the 1950s had round domes. The domes and all equipment were removed. The land was donated to the city of San Rafael and is known as Harry A. Barbier Memorial Park.

The Bayview Trail-Miwok Trail-Shoreline Trail is a less strenuous, 6-mile loop that climbs gently through mixed woodlands as it circles the Back Ranch Meadows Campground and Miwok Meadows. Enjoy the views along the way. The Bayview Trail begins near the campground entrance.

Marin County is thought to be named for the legendary Chief Marin, El Marinero, meaning "mariner" in Spanish. Mission records do show an Indian boatman name Marin, but whether he was a chief is not documented. The legend of Chief Marin leading his warriors against the Spanish and causing great havoc is an exciting story.

A less romantic theory on the name Marin comes from and abbreviated version of the Spanish name on the survey map made by Ayala in 1775. Today's San Rafael Bay was named on that map "Bahia de Neustra del Rosario, la Marinera," translated as "Bay of Our Lady of the Rosary, the Mariner." The name was shortened later simply to "Marin."

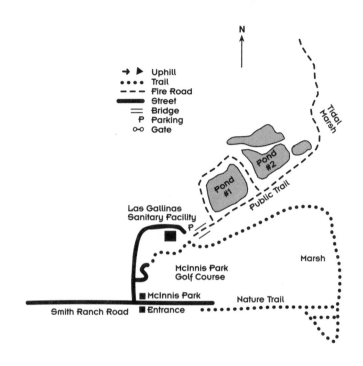

McInnis Park Marsh
McInnis County Park

ACCESS: Smith Ranch Road

POINTS OF INTEREST: Waterfowl, birds, views

DISTANCE: Marsh loop: 2.5 miles
                Public Trail (one way): 2 miles

DIFFICULTY: Easy

INFORMATION: McInnis Park
                  (415) 446-4423

McInnis Park Marsh
McInnis County Park

McInnis Park in Terra Linda offers recreational facilities and a trail that meanders through a marsh with wildlife and scenic views.

Beyond the soccer fields, softball diamonds, tennis courts, and golf course is a nature trail atop levees, which weaves along Las Gallinas Creek and loops around the golf course and through a salt marsh.

The path begins near the canoe launch and heads toward San Pablo Bay. If you're interested in birds, bring your binoculars. Great blue herons are frequent visitors to the marsh. Egrets, both great and snowy, can usually be seen walking or stalking the muddy edges of Las Gallinas Creek. Stilts probe the shallows, while gulls and terns sail back and forth over the water. Cormorants swim and dive for fish in the creek. Red-winged blackbirds like to perch in a line on an old section of fence while finches and other song birds flit in the small bushes, making it a challenge to focus the binoculars before they flutter to their next perch. Also watch for hawks and turkey vultures soaring overhead.

The great expanse of openness surrounded by Marin communities provides a pleasant respite from life's hustle and bustle. A 360-degree view encompasses the waters of San Pablo Bay extending to the Richmond hills. Mount Burdell rises to the north, Big Rock Ridge to the west, and San Pedro Mountain in the foreground to the south with Mt. Tamalpais in the distance.

The hike can be extended by exploring the Las Gallinas Ponds just to the north of McInnis Park. You can walk to the Public Trail along the ponds from the north end of the McInnis leeve trail. The Public Trail extends two miles along levees from the small parking lot near the Las Gallinas Valley Sanitary Facility. These ponds provide an excellent habitat for birds and ducks year round and the islands in the first pond are used by several species for nesting.

Spring provides a parade of babies, including Canada geese, mallard, heron, grebes, and at least a dozen other species of birds and waterfowl that nest on the islands or in the nearby marsh. Be sure to bring a pair of binoculars or a spotting scope for examining the islands and ducks in the center of the large pond.

Eldridge Grade
Marin Municipal Water District

ACCESS: Sky Oaks Road, off Fairfax-Bolinas Road

POINTS OF INTEREST: Views, wildflowers, wildlife

DISTANCE: Lake Lagunitas to Mt. Tam Summit round-trip:
       11 miles, moderate
       Colier Springs–Northside–Eldridge Grade–Lakeview:
       10 miles, strenuous

DIFFICULTY: Moderate, Strenuous

INFORMATION: Marin Municipal Water District Ranger Office
       (415) 945-1181

Eldridge Grade
Marin Municipal Water District

Eldridge Grade was a wagon road built by Chinese laborers in the late 1880s. Its gradual, zigzagging grade, which goes up to the summit of Mt. Tamalpais from the watershed lakes, makes it a popular route for those who want to climb Mt. Tam.

Lake Lagunitas to East Peak via Eldridge Grade is a moderately strenuous, 11-mile round-trip hike. Beginning at the Lake Lagunitas parking area, walk up the fire road on the left side of the dam and follow it past the lake. As you continue up the Lakeview Road and onto the Eldridge Grade, you begin to rise above the mixed forest of redwood, bay, oak, madrone, and Douglas fir. During the 1,800-foot elevation change between Lake Lagunitas and East Peak, you'll see forest dwindle into chaparral. Views grow more extensive along the way. To enjoy the views from Inspiration Point, take a 100-yard detour on the Northside Trail then return to Eldridge Grade.

When you reach the East Peak parking area, you have some options: you can circle the summit on the almost level .7-mile Verna Dunshee Trail and/or head sharply up the .5-mile Plankwalk Trail to the top of East Peak. The last 300-vertical-foot scramble up to the 2,571-foot summit on the Plankwalk Trail is merciless on tired legs that have just carried you 5.5 miles from Lake Lagunitas, but the satisfaction of having "climbed Mt. Tam" is a supreme prize.

The trek to the top of Mt. Tam can be even more challenging if you choose to make a loop by combining the Colier Springs Trail, Northside Trail, Eldridge Grade, and Lakeview Road. This route is shorter by about one mile, but it is strenuous because the Colier Springs Trail is steep.

Locate the Colier Springs Trail by walking about halfway around the south side of Lake Lagunitas and watching for a trail sign just past a footbridge. The trail winds sharply up beside the Middle Fork of Lagunitas Creek through a thick forest. During the spring, the creek cascades with white water splattering and splashing down the deeply carved ravine. At the intersection of trails at Colier Spring, turn left and follow the Northside Trail as it weaves through chaparral with vistas to the north. Join Eldridge Grade at Inspiration Point and continue to East Peak.

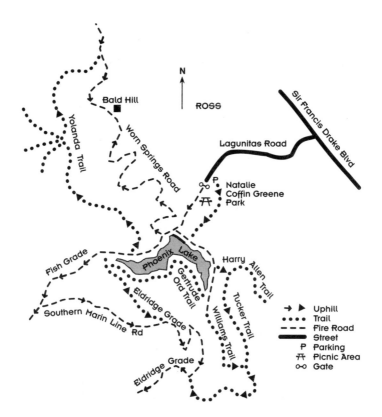

Phoenix Lake
Marin Municipal Water District

ACCESS: Laguitas Road through Natalie Coffin Greene Park

POINTS OF INTEREST: Wildflowers, views, fishing

DISTANCE: Phoenix Lake loop: 1.5 miles, easy
     Yolanda–Worn Springs: 4.5 miles, moderate
     Tucker Trail–Eldridge Grade: 3.5 miles, moderate

DIFFICULTY: Easy, Moderate

INFORMATION: Marin Municipal Water District Ranger Office
      (415) 945-1181

Phoenix Lake
Marin Municipal Water District

Phoenix Lake is probably the best known of all the Marin reservoirs. The original earthen dam was built in 1905. The lake's location, tucked deep into a ravine in the back of Ross, is easily reached. Access is through Natalie Coffin Greene Park, which provides about 25 parking spaces and a shaded picnic area.

The lake is small and easy to walk around, and offers redwood forest, oak woodlands, wildflowers, and plenty of good fishing spots. Phoenix Lake has been turned into a warm water fishery for bass and trout.

There are several main trails and fire roads that begin at or pass by Phoenix Lake. You can just walk around the lake or add one of several loops to extend your exploration. You can also use Phoenix Lake as a starting point for major hikes on watershed land with destinations including the Lake Lagunitas, Bon Tempe Lake, the Potrero picnic area, and the summit of Mt. Tamalpais.

The Yolanda Trail and Worn Springs Road create a moderately strenuous, 4.5-mile loop that winds up through shady oaks and across open grassland areas to the top of Bald Hill. From its rounded summit are excellent views of Ross and San Anselmo. The San Francisco Theological Seminary, built in 1892, looks like a stately castle. You can see downtown San Rafael and San Francisco Bay, the East Bay, and Mt. Diablo. Buildings in San Francisco and the fire lookout on Mt. Tam are also visible.

The Tucker Trail–Eldridge Grade loop journeys around the sides of Bill Williams Gulch through thick stands of redwood trees. Take the Harry Allen Trail up a short distance to the junction with the Tucker Trail. Turn right and follow the Tucker Trail as it weaves along the contour of the ridge. From the trail you can look down through the redwoods to Bill Williams Creek and trail.

Past the Bill Williams Trail junction, the Tucker Trail begins to climb. In this area was Tucker Camp, one of many hunters' camps sprinkled over Mt. Tam during the late 1800s. Turn right and head downhill at the Eldridge Grade junction. Part way down, Eldridge Grade veers off to the right and narrows to a trail. Follow it back to Phoenix Lake.

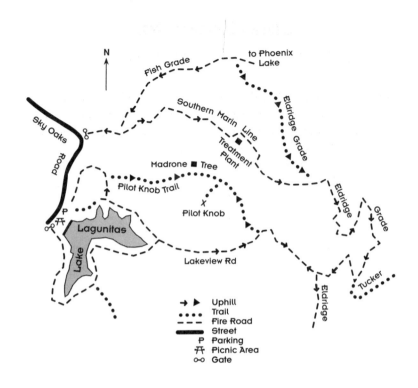

Lake Lagunitas
Marin Municipal Water District

ACCESS: Sky Oaks Road, off Fairfax-Bolinas Road

POINTS OF INTEREST: Wildflowers, views, fishing

DISTANCE: Lake Lagunitas loop: 1.5 miles, easy
Lakeview–Pilot Knob: 3 miles, easy
Lakeview–Eldridge Grade-Southern Marin
   Line: 4 miles, moderate

DIFFICULTY: Easy, Moderate

INFORMATION: Marin Municipal Water District Ranger Office
(415) 945-1181

Lake Lagunitas
Marin Municipal Water District

Lake Lagunitas, built in 1873, is the oldest of the Marin Municipal Water District reservoirs. From its central location, walks varying from a one-hour stroll around the lake to an all-day expedition to the summit of Mt. Tamalpais are possible.

A combination of fire roads and trails create a scenic trek around the lake. The trail journeys through grassland areas and thick forest with a mixture of redwood, bay, oak, madrone, and Douglas fir.

Fishing a popular activity at this lake as it is stocked with rainbow trout and large-mouth bass.

The Pilot Knob Trail is an interesting side hike that can be added to the Lake loop or explored separately. Begin the walk around the north side of the Lake, then head up the first fire road past the residential area and branch off onto the Pilot Knob Trail. This footpath meanders up through shady oak woodlands. Watch for a huge madrone tree just off the trail. Continue over the crest of the hill and down a gentle slope.

The Lakeview Road, Eldridge Grade and Southern Marin Line Road create an easy loop that features several view points. The Lakeview Road leaves Lake Lagunitas and heads up to a junction with Eldridge Grade. Go left and downhill at this junction and enjoy the view into the deep ravine of Bill Williams Creek. The homes at the top of Kent Woodlands come into view along with views of San Pablo Bay, San Pedro Ridge, and the Marin Islands. The Richmond Hills may be distinguishable, and on a clear day, Mt. Diablo will rise above all the East Bay ridges.

On the Southern Marin Line Road you will walk past the Marin Municipal Water District treatment plant. The road is paved from the treatment plant to Lake Lagunitas. You may see wildflowers along the roads. In late spring, watch for the delicate red larkspur that grow in protected spots. Moist areas nourish maidenhair ferns and horsetails. You'll know that summer is coming when you see the pretty pink blossoms of farewell to spring, which comes into bloom as the green grasses turn golden. The orange monkeyflowers continue to add their color well into summer.

Entrance fee is $5 per vehicle.

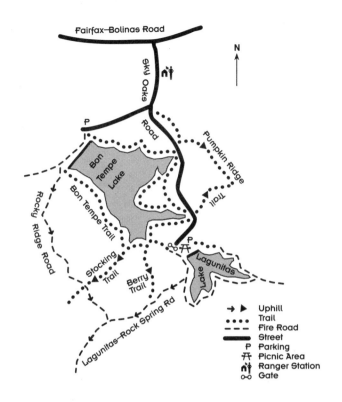

Bon Tempe Lake
Marin Municipal Water District

ACCESS: Sky Oaks Road, off Fairfax-Bolinas Road

POINTS OF INTEREST: Wildflowers, views, fishing

DISTANCE: Bon Tempe Lake loop: 4 miles, easy
Bon Tempe–Stocking–Rocky Ridge: 3 miles
Bon Tempe–Berry–Lagunitas-Rock Spring–
Rocky Ridge: 4 miles

DIFFICULTY: Easy, Moderate

INFORMATION: Marin Municipal Water District Ranger Office
(415) 945-1181

Bon Tempe Lake
Marin Municipal Water District

Bon Tempe Lake is one of the stair-step reservoirs in the Marin Municipal Water District watershed. Bon Tempe Trail is an easy, 4-mile loop with very little elevation change. Following the trail from the parking lot near the Lake Lagunitas spillway, you immediately plunge into deep forest mixed with large Douglas fir, bay, madrone, black oak, and a small redwood grove. Spring wildflowers on the shaded side of the lake include iris, hound's tongue, shooting star, and white milkmaid.

Cross the Bon Tempe dam and join the trail on the north side of the lake as it weaves through rolling grassland. Sun-loving wildflowers along this portion of the trail include owl's clover, buttercup, poppy, sky lupine, and Douglas iris.

A variety of ducks are usually visible out on the lake. Cormorants often stand like black statues drying their wings. Harder to spot are the great blue herons, who are almost invisible when they stand still along the shoreline. Grebes, mallards, and ruddy ducks are a few of the regulars that may be seen at the lake. Watch for turtles on partially submerged logs.

Osprey, beautiful black and white hawks, nest in the area during spring and summer. Osprey dive for a fish, dramatically plummeting feet first, then rise straight up from the water with their massive wings pumping and a fish clasped in their talons. When flying, osprey carry a fish head-first in an aerodynamic position.

Rocky Ridge Road, Stocking Trail, and Bon Tempe Trail combine to make an interesting loop. Hiking up the Rocky Ridge Fire Road, you climb the crest of the ridge; views extend over the watershed. The landscape is rocky and dominated by manzanita. Once on the Stocking Trail, you descend toward the lake.

Berry Trail–Lagunitas-Rock Spring Road-Rocky Ridge Road is another extension of the lake loop. The Berry Trail heads sharply up the forested ridge. Part way up, an opening in the trees allows you to take in the view of Bon Tempe's royal-blue pool framed by rolling hills. Turn right onto the Lagunitas-Rock Spring Road, then right again onto Rocky Ridge, which leads back to the lake.

Entrance fee is $5 per vehicle.

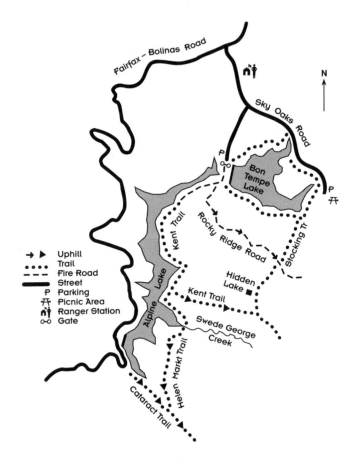

Alpine Lake
Marin Municipal Water District

ACCESS: Sky Oaks Road, off Fairfax-Bolinas Road

POINTS OF INTEREST: Wildflowers, waterfowl

DISTANCE: Kent-Helen Markt (one way): 3.5 miles

DIFFICULTY: Moderate

INFORMATION: Marin Municipal Water District Ranger Office
(415) 945-1181

Alpine Lake
Marin Municipal Water District

Alpine Lake is not as well known as its sister reservoirs, Bon Tempe, Lagunitas, and Phoenix. The fact that there is no loop path around Alpine Lake may be the reason the Kent Trail, which winds beside its eastern shore, is rarely crowded.

Begin the hike at the Bon Tempe Lake parking area. Walk across the Bon Tempe dam and turn right. Follow the fire road a short distance until it narrows into a trail skirting the Alpine Lake shoreline. This moderately strenuous footpath winds 3.5 miles to the junction of the Cataract Trail. You return via the same route.

The Kent Trail wanders through a fascinating mixture of landscapes. One moment you're trekking over serpentine outcroppings, two minutes later you're walking in a thick forest of Douglas fir and redwood. There is an unpredictable quality about this trail that keeps you wondering what lies around the next bend. At 1.7 miles into the hike, the Kent Trail veers away from the lake and heads up the ridge.

Continue on the Helen Markt Trail which stays near the water's edge to Swede George Creek. At the large creek, you cross a wonderfully constructed footbridge. In 1953, when this trail was being constructed, it was difficult to get lumber to Swede George Creek. So, they floated the logs across the lake to build the bridge. This is a nice spot for a lunch break. The Helen Markt Trail leaves the shoreline and climbs gradually up the hillside to the junction of the Cataract Trail. This part of the hike is through redwood forest.

In 1865 a sawmill was built in the vicinity of today's Alpine Dam. Evidence of the logging is visible along the trail. Large redwood stumps are circled by young trees that sprouted from the roots of the parent tree after it was cut down. Redwood trees were the preferred lumber tree. When they were gone, the loggers came back and cut the oak and fir trees. A glance through this second-growth forest reveals a uniform size of most of the trees, some of which are over 100 years old now. Blackened trunks and fire scars mark some of the trees. The last great fire to rage through this area happened in September 1945. It burned for seven days, consuming 20,000 acres from Stinson beach to Woodacre.

Entrance fee is $5 per vehicle.

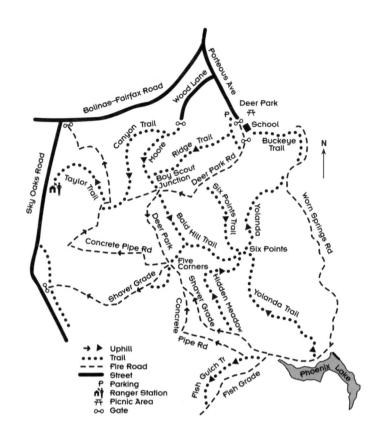

Deer Park Trailhead
Marin Municipal Water District

ACCESS: Porteous Avenue, off Fairfax-Bolinas Road

POINTS OF INTEREST: Views, wildflowers, wildlife

DISTANCE: Deer Park–Six Points–Bald Hill: 2.5 miles
Deer Park–Moore–Canyon: 2.5 miles
Deer Park–Concrete Pipe–Taylor–Shaver: 4 miles
Buckeye–Yolanda–Six Points–Deer Park: 3 miles

DIFFICULTY: Moderate

INFORMATION: Marin Municipal Water District Ranger Office
(415) 945-1181

Deer Park Trailhead
Marin Municipal Water District

Deer Park Trailhead in Fairfax offers access to a spider web of trails and fire roads weaving up ridges, around hills, and through small valleys and ravines.

Deer Park provides a picnic area, a restroom, and parking. There is a short nature trail that parallels the creek. To access the Deer Park Road, which is the main route for all major hikes from the trailhead, walk around the left side of the school building. The Deer Park Road begins at the gate just beyond the school.

A 2.5-mile loop created by Deer Park Road–Six Points Trail–Bald Hill Trail is an excellent introduction to the area. Begin by walking along the Deer Park Road and watch for the Six Points Trail, which goes off to the left. The footpath meanders through a thick forest of bay that line a creekbed. You pass through redwood groves and a serene little hollow before emerging at Six Points on the crest of the ridge. After enjoying the views of Mt. Tam and the many ridges, follow the Bald Hill Trail along the crest of the hill to Boy Scout Junction and return to the trailhead via the Deer Park Road. A variety of wildflowers decorate the hollows and hillsides in spring and early summer.

From Boy Scout Junction, a 1.5-mile loop can be created by walking the Canyon and Moore trails. At Boy Scout Junction, join the Moore Trail as it descends along the hillside. The Canyon Trail splits off the Moore Trail within sight of the Marin Stables. Then head back up the Canyon Trail, which follows a ravine.

Another adventurous hike is the Deer Park Road–Concrete Pipe Road–Taylor Trail–Shaver Grade loop. This 4-mile trek crosses a variety of landscapes including thick forest, grassland hillsides, and small meadows. The Taylor Trail emerges near the Sky Oaks Ranger Station. Walk along the Sky Oaks Road and veer off to the left on the Shaver Grade, which will lead you back to Five Corners where you connect with the Deer Park Road.

Buckeye Trail–Yolanda Trail–Six Points Trail–Deer Park Road makes a 3-mile loop that climbs the ridge via the Buckeye Trail, follows the shady Yolanda Trail, and descends the Six Points Trail to Deer Park Road.

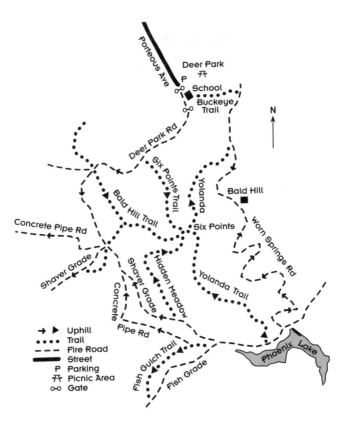

Legend:
- → ▶ Uphill
- •••• Trail
- - - - Fire Road
- ▬ Street
- P Parking
- ⚘ Picnic Area
- o—o Gate

Six Points
Marin Municipal Water District

ACCESS: Porteous Avenue, off Fairfax-Bolinas Road

POINTS OF INTEREST: Views, wildflowers, wildlife

DISTANCE: Deer Park–Six Points–Yolanda Trail–Shaver Grade–
             Hidden Meadow–Bald Hill: 5 miles
             Buckeye–Worn Springs–Yolanda–Six Points–
             Deer Park Road: 6.5 miles

DIFFICULTY: Moderate

INFORMATION: Marin Municipal Water District Ranger Office
                 (415) 945-1181

Six Points
Marin Municipal Water District

Many loop hikes are possible once you reach the Six Points junction, and you can choose the mileage and difficulty for your ability.

An excellent introductory hike to this area is the moderately strenuous, 5-mile loop that includes the Deer Park Road, Six Points Trail, Yolanda Trail, Shaver Grade, Hidden Meadow, Bald Hill Trail. Beginning at Deer Park Trailhead, head up the Six Points Trail and join the Yolanda Trail heading south. As you hike down the Yolanda Trail toward Phoenix Lake, notice the changing landscape. The open patches of rocky grassland and chaparral give way to mixed forest of live oak, black oak, buckeye, bay, and toyon trees. The steep mountainside above your left shoulder is the west side of Bald Hill. To the south, Mt. Tam's familiar profile graces the scenery. Below are deeply carved ravines with sharp forested ridges rising all around. When you arrive at Phoenix Lake, turn right and walk along the fire road, then follow Shaver Grade. Turn right onto Hidden Meadow Trail and hike along the seasonal creek and through the meadow that is a pallette of color during the wildflower bloom. Climb up to Six Points and return to Deer Park Road via Bald Hill Trail or retrace your steps on the Six Points Trail.

Bald Hill's summit offers a great place to enjoy lunch and grand views. Head up there on a 6.5-mile, moderately strenuous trek via the Buckeye Trail, Worn Springs Road, Yolanda Trail, Six Points Trail, and Deer Park Road. Begin on the Buckeye Trail, which veers off from the left side of the school and winds uphill to the fire road. Continue the climb up the steep section of the Worn Springs Road. Your efforts are rewarded with panoramic views from the summit, which include the San Francisco Theological Seminary, built in 1892, that looks like a stately castle. Downtown San Rafael, San Francisco Bay, San Francisco, and the fire lookout atop Mt. Tamalpais are also visible. Complete the loop by hiking down on the Worn Springs Road to Phoenix Lake and then winding up the Yolanda Trail to Six Points. Connect with the Six Points Trail to the Deer Park Road.

The name "Yolanda" comes from a small community that was between San Anselmo and Fairfax. The Yolanda Trail was built by the Civilian Conservation Corps in 1930.

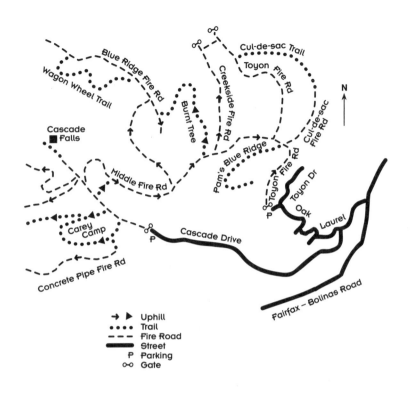

→ ▶	Uphill	
••••	Trail	
– – –	Fire Road	
▬▬	Street	
P	Parking	
o—o	Gate	

Cascade Canyon
Marin Open Space District

ACCESS: End of Cascade Drive, Oak Drive off Toyon Drive

POINTS OF INTEREST: Views, wildflowers, waterfall

DISTANCE: Cascade Falls: 1 mile, easy
           Middle–Blue Ridge–Burnt Tree: 3 miles, strenuous
           Toyon–Creekside–Middle: 3.5 miles, moderate

DIFFICULTY: Easy, Moderate, Strenuous

INFORMATION: Marin County Open Space
                 (415) 499-6405

Cascade Canyon
Marin Open Space District

Cascade Canyon Open Space in Fairfax encompasses a deep canyon with a creek, a waterfall, and an adjacent 1,000-foot Blue Ridge.

Cascade Falls is an easy 30-minute walk from the end of Cascade Drive. Water sheets over a large boulder and falls into a beautiful pool. The flow depends on the amount of recent rainfall.

Two loop trails weave around and to the top of two prominent peaks, the Blue Ridge summit and Pam's Blue Ridge. Access includes steep climbs excellent for hikers who desire challenging terrain. Some of the hillsides are heavily wooded with big-leaf maple, black oak, and bay trees.

Middle Fire Road–Blue Ridge Fire Road–Burnt Tree Trail makes a strenuous, 3-mile circle which is steep most of the way. The east and north sides of the ridge are wooded with oaks, Douglas fir, and madrone. On the south and west sides, the trails pass through chaparral. The summit is crowned with a rocky outcropping. There are no trees to obscure the sweeping view. From the ridge top, you can look out over the communities of Fairfax, San Anselmo, and San Rafael nestled into their respective valleys, and if the day is clear, you can see San Francisco Bay, the East Bay hills, and Mt. Diablo with surprising clarity.

The Toyon Fire Road–Creekside Fire Road–Middle Fire Road loop is a moderately strenuous 3.5 mile hike. The Toyon Fire Road is steep from the access on Toyon Drive up to the intersection with Cul-de-sac Fire Road. Continue to the next intersection and turn right on the Toyon Fire Road and follow it along the contour of the ridge. Turn left just before the boundary gate and head down on the Creekside Fire Road. This section of the hike parallels a creek which grows from a trickle to a steady flow as it tumbles down its rocky course during the winter and spring. Turn left onto Middle Fire Road and follow it uphill to the Toyon Fire Road.

Pam's Blue Ridge Trail, offers views as the path curves around the summit. A memorial plaque is atop Pam's Blue Ridge in memory of Pamela Prentice Ettinger, who died in an automobile accident.

The neighborhood streets are winding and narrow. Parking is very limited at the access points to Cascade Canyon Open Space.

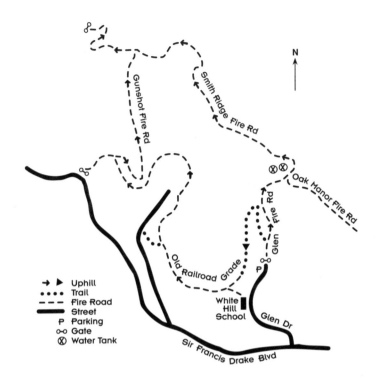

Legend:
- → ▶ Uphill
- •••• Trail
- – – – Fire Road
- ▬ Street
- P Parking
- ∞ Gate
- ⊗ Water Tank

Loma Alta
Marin Open Space District

ACCESS: End of Glen Drive, off Sir Francis Drake Blvd.

POINTS OF INTEREST: Views, wildflowers, seasonal streams

DISTANCE: Glen Fire Road–Smith Ridge–Gunshot–Old
Railroad Grade: 5 miles

DIFFICULTY: Strenuous

INFORMATION: Marin County Open Space
(415) 499-6405

Loma Alta
Marin Open Space District

Loma Alta Open Space, on the north side of Sir Francis Drake Boulevard as it passes over White's Hill, is a grassy ridge that offers panoramic views and a glimpse of Marin history.

A strenuous, 5-mile loop provides a tour of the ridge. Beginning at Glen Fire Road, follow Smith Ridge Fire Road to the open-space boundary near the summit and return via Gunshot Fire Road and Old Railroad Grade.

The first steps along the Glen Fire Road wind next to a stream that flows through a ravine thick with bay trees. Continue up the fire road to the two water tanks on Smith Saddle.

Pass the two tanks, stay left, and hike up the Smith Ridge Fire Road. On the long, steady climb, you pass several ravines crowded with bay, buckeye, and oaks. The reward for the uphill walking is superb vistas that feature central Marin, San Francisco Bay, Mt. Diablo, the San Francisco skyline, and Mt. Tamalpais.

Spring wildflowers on the sunny south-facing slope include pink shooting stars, orange poppies, yellow buttercups, blue brodiaea, blue-eyed grass, and purple vetch.

You may want to pass the intersection with the Gunshot Fire Road and continue to the dead end at the open-space boundary at top of the Smith Ridge where the views are superb. Back-track to Gunshot Fire Road when you're ready to descend. Gunshot Fire Road is steep and you'll descend quickly to the intersection with the Old Railroad Grade. The grade lessens as you walk along portions of Marin's historic railroad line. Trestles and two tunnels were originally constructed by the North Pacific Coast Railroad in 1874 to get trains over White's Hill. The Old White's Hill Grade, as it was known, was used until 1904 when a bypass was built that included a longer tunnel at a lower elevation, shortening the route by 2 miles.

Today, the fire road that follows the Old Railroad Grade, weaves around the heads of deep canyons that were once spanned by large wooden trestles. During winter and spring a beautiful waterfall cascades down the steep ravine above Baywood Canyon.

Near the end of the loop, the trail narrows, meanders through a forested ravine, and connects with the Glen Fire Road.

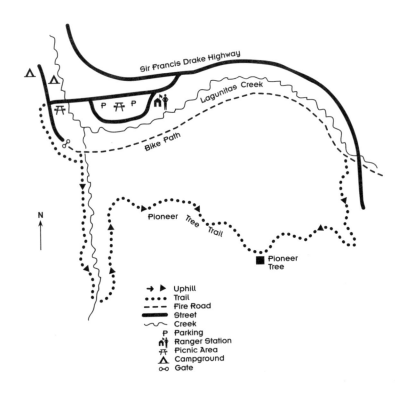

Pioneer Tree Trail
Samuel P. Taylor State Park

ACCESS: Sir Francis Drake Highway

POINTS OF INTEREST: Redwood groves, wildflowers

DISTANCE: Pioneer Tree Trail loop: 3.5 miles

DIFFICULTY: Easy

INFORMATION: Samuel P. Taylor State Park
                 (415) 488-9897

Pioneer Tree Trail
Samuel P. Taylor State Park

The Pioneer Tree Trail, when joined with the bike path that runs through the park, creates a 3.5-mile loop that meanders alongside a creek and through a dense redwood forest.

The trail begins near the group picnic area. Within a few minutes, the path leads deep into a canyon alongside a seasonal creek that gushes over cascades and debris in the winter and spring and continues with a dribble from pool to pool throughout most of the summer.

The path curves away from the creek and follows a gentle sloping grade up the hillside. Brilliant beams of sunlight stream through openings in the canopy, illuminating thimbleberry leaves. The fluorescent green hue of the leaves, some surrounded by a golden halo effect, give the dark forest a magical appearance.

Watch for the twin redwoods on the left side of the path. The barks of the two huge trees actually merge near the ground. They are amazingly identical in height, girth, and overall shape, and they even have matching fire scars in their trunks.

As the trail follows a contour around the hill, it passes the Pioneer Tree. This cluster of trees is an excellent example of the circle-of-life reproduction of redwood trees. In the center of six younger trees is a giant parent tree. Even though redwood trees produce cones with seeds capable of growing new trees, sprouts growing from the base of a parent tree represent the most common form of reproduction. The sprouts grow rapidly, nourished by the established root system. The circular arrangement, with many intermingled root systems, creates a strong base for the tall trees that can reach two hundred feet in height.

Continue on the trail as it zigzags down through a less dense landscape. Notice that the forest has changed. This side of the hill is drier and there are more Douglas firs and oaks than redwoods.

The Pioneer Tree Trail ends at the junction of the bike path (fire road) near the bicycle bridge that spans the street. Turn left and enjoy the walk back to the main picnic area on the bike path as it parallels Lagunitas Creek. Glance frequently down at creek for possible sightings of wildlife.

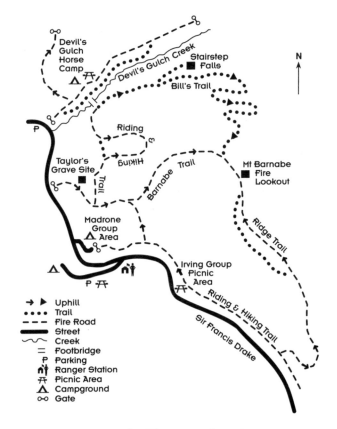

Mt. Barnabe
Samuel P. Taylor State Park

ACCESS: Sir Francis Drake Highway

POINTS OF INTEREST: Views, wildflowers, wildlife

DISTANCE: Riding & Hiking–Ridge–Barnabe loop: 7 miles
Bill's–Barnabe–Riding & Hiking loop: 5 miles

DIFFICULTY: Moderate

INFORMATION: Samuel P. Taylor State Park
(415) 488-9897

Mt. Barnabe
Samuel P. Taylor State Park

This 5-mile loop will take you to the 1,466-foot summit of Mt. Barnabe. Views along the way and from the top are extensive. A fire lookout station, operated by the Marin County Fire Department, has occupied the peak since 1940.

Mt. Barnabe might be the only mountain ever named for a mule. Barnabe was the Taylor children's pet. He was a white army mule said to have come to California with Col. John C. Fremont's men in the 1840s. Barnabe loved to graze on the mountain and reportedly knew how to open every gate between himself and his favorite spots. Whenever he wandered off, the children knew where to find him.

Beginning at the Irving Group Picnic Area, join the Riding & Hiking Trail and go south as it parallels Sir Francis Drake Highway. Turn left onto the Ridge Trail, which is a fire road. The grade begins immediately and goes up steadily all the way to the top.

While walking along the crest on the Ridge Trail, you can see the San Geronimo Valley and the community of Lagunitas to the east. Joseph Warren Revere (the grandson of Paul Revere) owned this valley in the late 1840s. Lagunitas already had some summer cabins in it when the railroad built its line through the valley in 1874. As you approach the top, glance back to the south to see Peters Dam, completed in 1953. It holds back the water of Kent Lake. Continue the loop, by walking down the Barnabe Trail and taking two left turns to return to the Irving Group Picnic Area.

Bill's Trail offers a shady route to the summit. Enter Devil's Gulch, cross the creek via the footbridge, and go left onto Bill's Trail. This path zigzags up the forested side of Mt. Barnabe. You can see Stairstep Falls by taking the short spur trail.

From the summit, the fire lookout on the top of Mt. Tamalpais is visible over the ridges in the foreground. Mt. Diablo can be seen directly east.

There are no facilities at the summit, so plan for a picnic on the ground. The views are primarily to the west and north. Two forested ridges stand between you and the Pacific Ocean. The second ridge is Point Reyes. Tomales Bay fills the basin between the rolling grasslands and the forested Inverness Ridge.

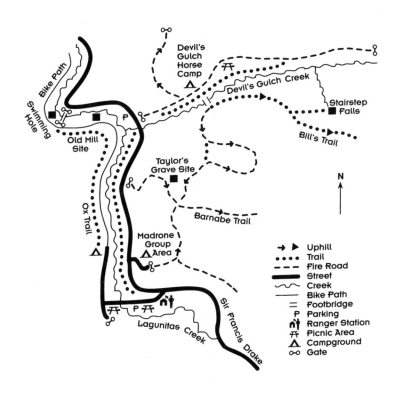

Devil's Gulch
Samuel P. Taylor State Park

ACCESS: Sir Francis Drake Highway

POINTS OF INTEREST: Wildflowers, wildlife, seasonal waterfall

DISTANCE: Devil's Gulch (one way): 2 miles
Stairstep Falls side trip: 1 mile

DIFFICULTY: Easy

INFORMATION: Samuel P. Taylor State Park
(415) 488-9897

Devil's Gulch
Samuel P. Taylor State Park

Devil's Gulch follows part of an ancient Indian path that crossed Marin County. In those days, the trail was a torturous route, and this is reflected in its name. Today, however, it's an easy walk on a creekside trail and smooth fireroad. Well known for its wide variety of wildflowers in the spring and beautiful deep forest setting, it is one of the most popular hikes in the park.

About half a mile into the gulch is a clearing with a horse corral and picnic area. This is thought to be the location of a dairy that served the tiny community of Taylorville in the late 1800s. The clearing stretches on about another half mile. Near the far end is the former location of one of the Taylor sons' home and orchard. Nothing remains of the house, but a few pear trees still stand.

The gulch area is a botanist's delight. The cool, moist conditions yield a variety of plants — from the common hound's tongues, milkmaids and buttercups to the less common columbines, mission bells, bleeding hearts, and creek dogwood. These conditions also provide the opportunity to see rarer plants such as orchids and California nutmeg trees. Seeing the complete pageant of wildflowers, would require numerous visits between January and August, as some plants have short blooming periods.

A visit to Stairstep Falls during the winter and spring is a delightful side trip. Cross the creek at the footbridge, turn left, and follow Bill's Trail as it parallels Devil's Gulch Creek and works its way up a gentle grade. Veer left onto the Stairstep Falls Trail and continue until you see the frothy ribbon sheeting and tumbling 40 feet down the steep slope.

While ambling along Devil's Gulch Creek in winter and early spring, watch for spawning salmon and trout. It's fascinating to watch these fish overcome obstacles in their trek upstream from the ocean to lay their eggs. The fish rest in pools, then suddenly burst forth with tremendous energy to thrash violently over the rocks or against strong currents to reach the next pool and rest again. This process is repeated until they find the place where they were hatched. The female deposits her eggs in shallow gravel areas and the male fertilizes them.

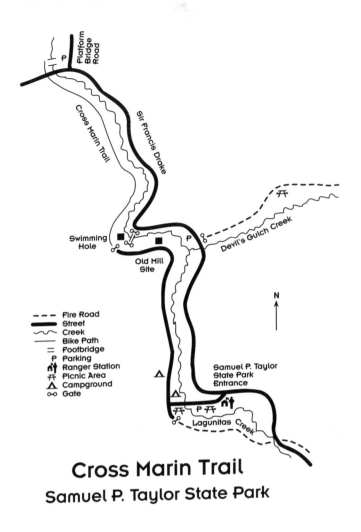

Legend:
- – – – Fire Road
- —— Street
- ～～ Creek
- —— Bike Path
- = Footbridge
- P Parking
- 🛉 Ranger Station
- ⛱ Picnic Area
- △ Campground
- ∞ Gate

Cross Marin Trail
Samuel P. Taylor State Park

ACCESS: Intersection of Platform Bridge Road and Sir Francis Drake Highway

POINTS OF INTEREST: Creekside path, historical sites

DISTANCE: Cross Marin Trail (one way): 4 miles

DIFFICULTY: Easy

INFORMATION: Samuel P. Taylor State Park
(415) 488-9897

Cross Marin Trail
Samuel P. Taylor State Park

The Cross Marin Trail is a paved path that weaves 4 miles from the intersection of Platform Bridge Road and Sir Francis Drake Highway to Samuel P. Taylor State Park. This level path provides an excellent year-round outing. It's shaded and cool during the warm months and provides a mudless hike during the rainy season.

Begin at Platform Bridge Road, about 4 miles west of the entrance to Samuel P. Taylor State Park. Cross the old bridge to see the paved Cross Marin Trail, which starts on the west side of the creek.

The trail parallels Lagunitas (Papermill) Creek. This quiet stream, less than twelve inches deep most of the year, can swell to several feet deep during wet season. Winter is the time to watch for salmon and trout swimming upstream to spawn.

The path follows the old railroad grade, which was built in 1879. The railroad line ran from central Marin to Point Reyes Station. In 1976, the Cross Marin Trail was paved as part of the Pacific Coast Bicentennial Bike Route.

The oak and bay forest along the creek merges into a dense grove of redwood trees as you near the heart of the Samuel P. Taylor State Park. Within the park boundaries are picnic tables, restrooms, drinking fountains, and historic sites.

Samuel Penfield Taylor settled on this land just after the California gold rush. He built a paper mill and a powder mill on the banks of Lagunitas Creek. Mill employees formed the small community of Taylorville. When the railroad pushed its line through this canyon, Taylor built a resort hotel and created Camp Taylor. In the late 1880s, it was a popular outing for people from San Francisco to cross to Marin and ride the train to West Marin. Many visitors stopped at Camp Taylor to enjoy camping, swimming, and hiking.

After you cross into the park, watch for signs marking the foundation of the old paper mill and an exhibit with old photographs of the mill and Taylorville. Next you will pass the dam site; the dam created a small lake that provided year-round water for the papermill. The Camp Taylor hotel was located in the middle of the park's main picnic area. All that remains of the old hotel is the circular cement fish pond that stands among the picnic tables.

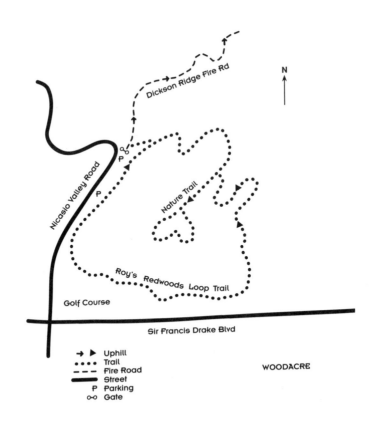

N

Dickson Ridge Fire Rd

Nicasio Valley Road

Nature Trail

Roy's Redwoods Loop Trail

Golf Course

Sir Francis Drake Blvd

→ ▶ Uphill
•••• Trail
– – – Fire Road
▬▬ Street
P Parking
o–o Gate

WOODACRE

Roy's Redwoods
Marin Open Space District

ACCESS: Nicasio Valley Road, off of Sir Francis Drake Blvd.

POINTS OF INTEREST: Redwood groves, wildflowers

DISTANCE: Roy's Redwoods Loop Trail: 2.5 miles, moderate
Nature Trail: .5 mile, easy

DIFFICULTY: Easy, Moderate

INFORMATION: Marin County Open Space
(415) 499-6405

76

Roy's Redwoods
Marin Open Space District

The grove of giant redwoods in Roy's Redwoods, located in San Geronimo Valley, offers a shady place for a picnic, a short nature walk, and interesting hiking trails that meander around a small hill. Beginning at the entrance gate near the restroom, you immediately enter a hollow with redwood trees surrounding a small meadow. This meadow and surrounding grove are excellent areas for children to explore. As you wander through the grove, note the sizes of the trees. Mature redwoods that are about 200 feet tall, are several hundred years old.

Redwoods are named for the color of their bark and heartwood. Tannic acid rather than sap flows within a redwood and provides resistance to fungi and insect infestation. The thick, fibrous bark helps insulate redwoods from fires. Redwood trees can live more than two thousand years.

Black fire scars are visible on the largest trees in the grove. You can estimate when the last fire might have swept through the area by finding a younger tree that has no black scars on its bark and guessing its age.

Examine the huge fallen redwood. Does it appear to have fallen a long time ago or just recently? Because of its natural resistance to fungus, this tree may lie on the ground for a hundred years before it decomposes.

The Roy's Redwoods Loop Trail is a 2.5-mile, hiking trail. Head uphill at the north end of the grove and join a well-used horse trail. Turn right and follow this trail over a saddle in the small ridge. For an interesting addition, explore the Nature Trail that branches off of the main path. This is a short loop that encircles the hilltop right above the redwood grove. It is a shady walk through a mixture of trees with spring and summer flowers.

Rejoin Roy's Redwoods Loop Trail and continue to the right zigzagging down through a forest of oak, Douglas fir, and bay trees with sword ferns and spring wildflowers.

The name Roy's Redwoods comes from Thomas and James Roy, who owned the property for 80 years dating back to 1877. They had a dairy ranch and operated a mill at the foot of Nicasio Hill.

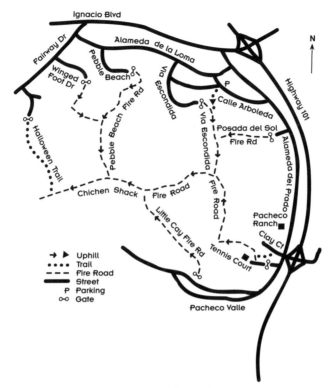

Loma Verde
Marin Open Space District

ACCESS: Calle Arboleda, Via Escondida, Clay Court

POINTS OF INTEREST: Views, wildflowers, wildlife

DISTANCE: Chicken Shack (one way): 3 miles
        Tennis Court–Via Escondida–Chicken Shack–
        Little Cay–Alameda del Prado loop: 3 miles

DIFFICULTY: Moderate

INFORMATION: Marin County Open Space
        (415) 499-6405

Loma Verde
Marin Open Space District

Scenic views highlight a hike on the Loma Verde Open Space Preserve, the ridge between Ignacio and Pacheco Valle in Novato. There are several access points on both sides of the ridge. They all begin with short, steep climbs to reach the Chicken Shack Fire Road that runs along the ridge top. Once you reach the crest, about 3 miles of fire roads and trails etch the preserve.

A mixed oak woodland covers the ridge. The deciduous black oaks and valley oaks are numerous. Buckeye trees are easy to identify in the fall with their nutlike seeds in light green casings dangling from their branches. In late fall and winter, reddish-orange berries hang in clusters on some of the madrone branches. Red toyon berries add winter color. The manzanita is identified by its small leaves and deep purple bark. Spring wildflowers provide a sprinkling of rainbow colors on the hill sides.

When you reach the crest of the ridge, head west. Views begin almost immediately. Peering through the trees to the north, you can see homes in Ignacio in the foreground and Mt. Burdell in the distance. To the east is Highway 101 with Hamilton Field occupying the land between the highway and the bay.

The Chicken Shack Fire Road atop the ridge levels out in spots to give you a chance to catch your breath. Continuing west, however, the grade climbs and the ridge narrows to barely wider than the fire road. From there you can see down into Pacheco Valle and then glance toward downtown Novato with a mere pivot of the head.

The higher the elevation, the better the view. Santa Venetia and the mouth of Las Gallinas Creek fill the lowland at the base of San Pedro Mountain. Mt. Tam's peak juts above other ridges to the south, and buildings in San Francisco are visible.

The open-space land borders private land, some of which is part of the historic Pacheco Ranch, still run by descendants of the original landowner. In 1840, Ignacio Pacheco, a sergeant in the Mexican army, was given the 6,600-acre Rancho San Jose land grant. The large Victorian home, visible from Highway 101, was built in 1881 by Pacheco's son. Today, grapes cover much of the Pacheco Ranch land.

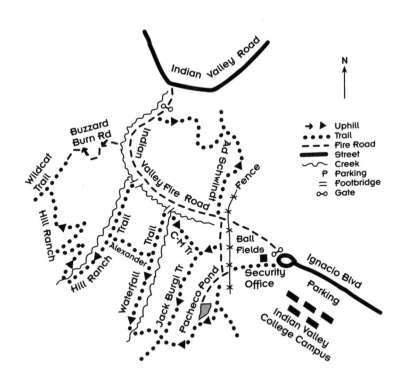

Indian Valley
Marin Open Space District

ACCESS: Ignacio Blvd. on the Indian Valley College Campus

POINTS OF INTEREST: Waterfall, pond, wildflowers, views

DISTANCE: Buzzard Burn–Wildcat–Hill Ranch: 2 miles, strenuous
   Waterfall–Pacheco Pond loop: 1.5 miles, moderate
   Ad Schwindt Trail–Indian Valley loop:1.5 miles, easy

DIFFICULTY: Easy, Moderate, Strenuous

INFORMATION: Marin County Open Space
   (415) 499-6405

Indian Valley
Marin Open Space District

Indian Valley Open Space in Novato has trails that loop over hills, wander along streams, and wind up ravines through a serene oak woodland setting. Numerous loop hikes varying from 1 to 4 miles can be created.

The main access to this open space is the Indian Valley College parking lot. Drive into the campus and follow the street until it dead-ends in a circle at the Campus Security Office. A $1 parking fee (bring four quarters) is required when classes are in session. Walk to the right of the Security Office past the ball fields and restrooms to the open-space gate.

The Buzzard Burn Fire Road and Hill Ranch Trail combine to make a strenuous 2-mile loop. Locate the Buzzard Burn Fire Road by going through the open-space boundary gate beyond the ball fields. Continue on the Indian Valley Fire Road past two wooden footbridges and climb steeply up the Buzzard Burn Fire Road. The wide road becomes a footpath near the top of the hill. Watch for the Hill Ranch Trail sign marking the path on the left. The Hill Ranch Trail zigzags down the hill and crosses the headwaters of two creeks on its way back to the Indian Valley Fire Road.

The Waterfall Trail–Pacheco Pond Fire Road loop is a popular 1.5-mile hike with a seasonal waterfall and a small reservoir. The deep forest makes this a lovely year-round hike with the cascading waterfall and stream in the winter, wildflowers in spring, and shady coolness during summer and fall.

Combining the Ad Schwindt Trail and Indian Fire Road creates a 1.5-mile loop that meanders around a small knob and along a ravine on the north side of the Indian Valley Fire Road. The forest is mostly oak and bay trees along this section.

Once you become familiar with the major loop trails, you can get creative. Explore the Alexander Trail, which veers off to the right just above the waterfall and climbs via a winding path up and over the hill between the Waterfall Trail and the Hill Ranch Trail.

The Jack Burgi Trail and the Clark-Melone Trail both etch the small ridge and provide variations to the Waterfall Trail–Pacheco Pond loop.

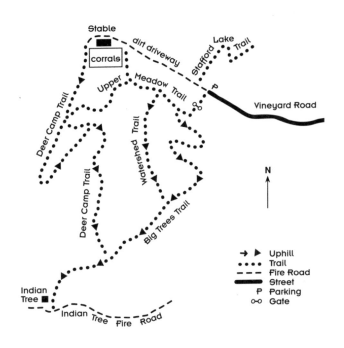

Indian Tree
Marin Open Space District

ACCESS: End of pavement on Vineyard Road

POINTS OF INTEREST: Giant redwoods, views, wildflowers

DISTANCE: Big Trees Trail to Indian Tree (one way): 3 miles
Big Trees–Deer Camp–Upper Meadow loop: 5.5 miles

DIFFICULTY: Moderate

INFORMATION: Marin County Open Space
(415) 499-6405

Indian Tree
Marin Open Space District

Redwood groves in Novato? Yes! Indian Tree Open Space Preserve in Novato features groves of redwood trees on Big Rock Ridge and and an especially interesting group of trees on the ridge top.

Park along Vineyard Road near the spot where the pavement ends. Begin the hike at the open-space gate and walk on the Upper Meadow Trail for a short distance. At the first trail split, go left up the Big Trees Trail, which is a 3-mile hike and a 1,300-foot climb to the giant redwood trees on the ridge top. You'll pass through dense bay forest mixed with some oaks and a little ground vegetation. The deep ravines funnel moisture which nurtures redwood trees lower on the ridge. Seeds from the redwoods on the summit may have washed down the seasonal streams and given birth to the trees in the lower groves. The redwoods hug the ravines for year-round moisture and protection from hot summer sun.

As the trail temporarily leaves the trees and crosses the open hillside, it provides a view of Stafford Lake, the Indian Valley Golf Course, and the entire valley surrounding Novato.

Oaks are the most numerous trees on the drier areas of the ridge. A mixture of madrone, bay, and toyon trees also grow on the hillside. Shortly after the appearance of Douglas fir trees, you enter a cool, dark redwood grove complete with lush undergrowth of huckleberry bushes and sword ferns. Some of the redwoods are large and quite old. They probably escaped the logger's saws because the grove was small and hard to reach.

The name "Indian Tree" is from a legend that says an Indian once lived in a hollowed-out giant redwood on the top of this ridge.

The location of the redwood trees, on the north side of the ridge, protects them from the hot summer sun. Fog often pushes in from the ocean through the gap in the hills to the west and provides the moisture the redwoods need.

For the trek down, follow the Deer Camp Trail, which exits through the group of buildings surrounding the stables, or veer off onto the Upper Meadow Trail to complete a 5.5-mile loop.

Seasonal note: During the wet season portions of certain trails may be closed to prevent erosion. Alternate routes are available.

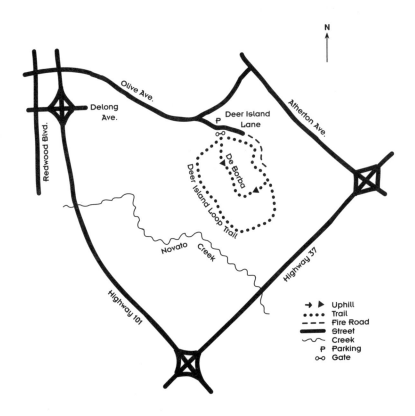

Deer Island
Marin Open Space District

ACCESS: Deer Island Lane, off Olive Avenue

POINTS OF INTEREST: Views, wildflowers, wildlife

DISTANCE: Deer Island Loop Trail: 1.8 miles
　　　　　De Borba Trail: 1 mile

DIFFICULTY: Easy

INFORMATION: Marin County Open Space
　　　　　　(415) 499-6405

Deer Island
Marin Open Space District

Today, Deer Island is a hill rising out of the marshes of Novato. It is not difficult, however, to imagine back to the time when the San Pablo Bay tides must have washed up against it.

The Deer Island Loop Trail circles the island providing an easy, 1.8-mile walk. Wildflowers are ablaze along the trail in the spring. Huge old bay and oak trees shade about half of the island. Open areas render views in all directions, framed with the yellows of sun cup, buttercup, and false lupine. Watch for the delicate pinks of hedge nettle and owl's clover. See how red clover and orange fiddleneck complement the bright blues of iris and lupine on the hillsides.

Your presence may be announced by crows and scrub jays perched in the tops of trees. You may hear the pretty song of the meadowlark, with its bright yellow chest and black triangle necklace, or marvel at the intense red shoulder patches on the red-winged blackbirds. The barn swallows put on quite a show — between swoops they seem to flip flop in the air, changing directions instantly. This is their feeding behavior; they catch and eat flying insects. These swallows fly so fast it's hard to get a good look at them, but their forked tails make them easy to identify.

Many animals call Deer Island their home. Watch dusty spots on the trail for footprints of deer or raccoon. Animal droppings (called scats) give clues to who roams the area at night. Brown pellets are rabbit, black pellets are deer. Raccoon scat may be filled with seed hulls. A bobcat scat will have lots of hair in it. Fox droppings have hair and bones from a diet of rodents and small mammals.

As you round the southeast end of the island, the water treatment ponds come into view. Beyond them is Highway 37. Continuing southwest along the trail, you see can Novato Creek and the marsh surrounding it. This low-lying area is an important habitat for birds and small mammals. Overhead, an assortment of hawks soar back and forth, ever watchful for prey on the ground.

The 1-mile De Borba Trail winds to Deer Island's summit and angles north and down the hill to join the loop trail.

Buildings on the northwest side of the island were part of an old dairy. Today, the house is a ranger residence.

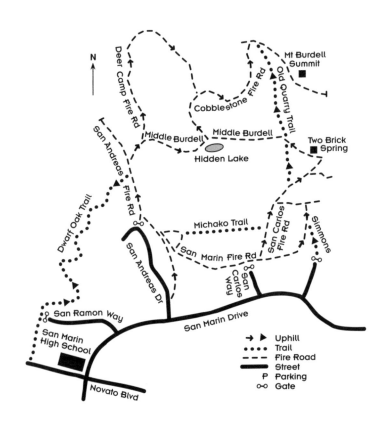

Mt. Burdell (West)
Marin Open Space District

ACCESS: San Andreas Drive, off of San Marin Drive

POINTS OF INTEREST: Views, wildflowers, wildlife

DISTANCE: Dwarf Oak Trail: 1.5 miles, easy
         San Andreas Drive to summit (one way): 2.7 miles
         San Andreas–Middle Burdell–Deer Camp: 3 miles

DIFFICULTY: Easy, Moderate

INFORMATION: Marin County Open Space
              (415) 499-6405

Mt. Burdell (West)
Marin Open Space District

Approximately 15 miles of fire roads and trails crisscross Mt. Burdell and wind up to its 1,500-foot summit. Views from the top are rewarding. A trail at the summit connects to the trails on Olompali State Historic Park located on the north slope of Mt. Burdell.

The Dwarf Oak Trail on the western side of Mt. Burdell offers a variety of landscapes and scenic views. Begin the hike at the open-space gate on San Andreas Drive. Follow the San Andreas Fire Road up the hill a quarter mile to the large meadow. Turn left, go through the cattle gate. This footpath meanders downhill for 1.5 miles to San Marin High School and ends at Novato Boulevard.

The San Andreas, Middle Burdell, and Cobblestone fire roads combine to create a popular route to the summit. This 2.7-mile (one way) hike is a steady climb on well-graded roads to the 1,500-foot peak. Along the way, you'll pass through oak woodland and open grassland areas.

The Michako Trail–San Carlos Fire Road–Middle Burdell Fire Road–San Andreas Fire Road make a nice 3-mile loop that crosses a variety of landscapes. You'll see bay trees crowded into ravines, oak trees dotting the hillsides, and spring wildflowers. Two Brick Spring is one of the natural springs on Mt. Burdell.

Hidden Lake is so hidden you may not notice it. It was created by a landslide that formed a hollow that filled with rain. Early Novato residents remember swimming in Hidden Lake. Today, it is a marshy area with a small pond during the rainy season.

San Andreas–Middle Burdell–Deer Camp fire roads create a 3-mile loop walk through open grassland with a few old oaks. In the spring, this area offers a lovely display of wildflowers, including delicate pink owl's clover, buttercup, poppy, iris, common brodiaea, blue-eyed grass, and lots of fiddleneck.

Mt. Burdell was part of the original Rancho Olompali land grant given to Camillo Ynitia in 1852. Ynitia was the only Indian in Marin to receive a land grant. Ynitia sold most of his land to James Black. When Black's daughter, Mary, married Galen Burdell in 1865, the Rancho Olompali land, including Mt. Burdell, was given to them as a wedding present.

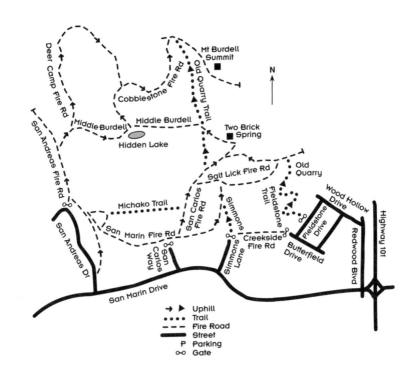

Mt. Burdell (East)
Marin Open Space District

ACCESS: End of Simmons Lane

POINTS OF INTEREST: Views, wildflowers, old rock quarry

DISTANCE: Creekside–Fieldstone–Middle Burdell–Salt Lick–
San Marin–Simmons: 2.5 miles

DIFFICULTY: Moderate

INFORMATION: Marin County Open Space
(415) 499-6405

Mt. Burdell (East)
Marin Open Space District

Hiking on the east side of Mt. Burdell features acres of rolling grassland, scenic views, and a curiously overgrown rock quarry.

A 2.5-mile loop hike that climbs 400 feet in elevation can be created by combining the Creekside Fire Road, Fieldstone Trail, Middle Burdell Fire Road, Salt Lick Fire Road, San Marin Fire Road and Simmons Trail. Beginning at the open-space gate on Simmons Lane, walk along the Creekside Fire Road to Butterfield Drive in the nearby neighborhood. Turn left onto Fieldstone Drive and walk half a block to the open-space gate that marks the start of the Fieldstone Trail. The Fieldstone Trail is footpath that zigzags up Mt. Burdell's eastern slope. Amid the flowing grassland, speckled with spring wildflowers, are large oak and bay trees.

Unlike many wooded areas in Marin that have become overgrown with masses of trees and shrubs, Mt. Burdell features fully developed trees separated by open areas. The absence of shrubs creates a picturesque effect both in the winter and spring, when grass is a green carpet, and in summer and autumn, when the golden grasses stretch across the hills. Several factors contribute to today's uncluttered landscape, including burning of the grass by Indians, almost constant grazing by cattle for over 130 years, and periodic droughts. The cattle that graze on Mt. Burdell today help trim the grass to reduce fire danger. They also nibble new shoots discouraging the growth of young trees and shrubs.

The old rock quarry is a curious sight. If hikers didn't know about it, they would surely wonder what had caused the heaps of rock that alternate with pits, long troughs, and deep gouges in the land. In contrast to the open hillsides, the quarry area has abundant undergrowth and is choked with shrubs and young trees. The rocky debris and unsure footing in the quarry may serve as a natural barrier to the cattle.

At the trail junction, follow the Middle Burdell Fire Road a short distance, pass through the cattle gate, then head down the Salt Lick Fire Road and down the San Marin Fire Road. As you descend Mt. Burdell's south-facing slope, the views encompass central Novato. Veer to the left onto the Simmons Trail to complete the loop hike.

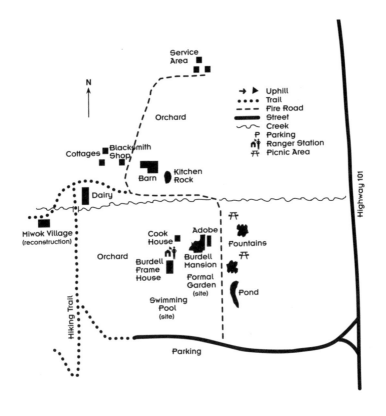

Olompali History Walk
Olompali State Historic Park

ACCESS: From southbound lane of Highway 101, 3 miles north of Novato

POINTS OF INTEREST: Historic buildings, flowers

DISTANCE: Historic area: 1 mile

DIFFICULTY: Easy

INFORMATION: Olompali State Historic Park
(415) 892-3383

Olompali History Walk
Olompali State Historic Park

In 1852, the Miwok leader Camillo Ynitia sold most of his Rancho Olompali to James Black. When Black's daughter Mary married San Francisco dentist Galen Burdell in 1865, the Rancho Olompali land was given to them as a wedding gift. The Burdells built a clapboard house that enclosed the old Indian adobe within its walls. Mary and Galen lived in the clapboard home until their deaths around 1900.

Rancho Olompali was a cattle ranch when the Burdells received it, and they developed it into a thriving business and beautiful estate. The fields were cultivated in grapes, fruit trees, and grains, and the property was highlighted by a huge formal garden. The hillside land was roamed by a large herd of cattle.

Galen Burdell was retired for most of the years he was at Olompali. He had an inventive and inquiring mind and was very interested in agriculture. He experimented with as many as 30 varieties of grapes. His extensive orchards included apple, pear, plum, orange, apricot, persimmon, pomegranate, walnut, and even banana trees. Mary created the magnificent garden that spread over four acres around the house and down terraces. Brick pathways wandered around fountains and through formal flower beds. When Mary traveled, she brought back exotic plants for her garden.

The Burdell Rancho continued its prosperity throughout the lifetime of their son James Burdell. He built the 26-room stucco mansion in 1911. His parents' clapboard house was torn down during construction of the mansion, but a wing of the new home was designed to enclose the old adobe. After James's death, his wife sold Olompali out of the Burdell Family.

In the 1950s, the University of San Francisco Jesuits owned Olompali and made it into a religious retreat. They added several structures, including the swimming pool and bath house, modern dairy, and caretaker's house. A hippie commune occupied Olompali from 1960 to 1969, when a fire destroyed much of the Burdell mansion. The fire revealed the historic old adobe, still standing.

The State of California purchased Olompali as an historic site in 1977. A structure with windows was built around the old adobe to protect it from the weather.

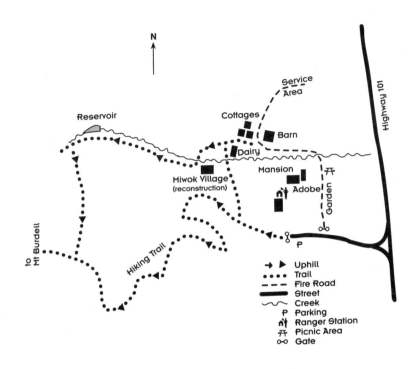

Olompali Hiking Trails
Olompali State Historic Park

ACCESS: From southbound lane of Highway 101, 3 miles north of Novato

POINTS OF INTEREST: flowers, historic buildings

DISTANCE: Hiking Trail loop: 2.5 miles
Hiking Trail to summit of Mt. Burdell: 5 miles

DIFFICULTY: Moderate

INFORMATION: Olompali State Historic Park
(415) 892-3383

Olompali Hiking Trails
Olompali State Historic Park

A 2.5-mile hiking trail winds up the north side of Mt. Burdell and loops back through the historic property. Spring wildflowers such as blue larkspur, shooting stars, and iris grow along the trail.

During the first mile of the path, several view points offer panoramas of the Rancho that once had cultivated fields and orchards and grazing herds of cattle. The trail zigzags up the hillside along a forested ravine. To complete the loop, veer off to the right at the trail junction and head downhill through bay and oak forest, past the small reservoir. As you walk through the meadow, stop and examine structures of the reconstructed Miwok Village.

For a 5-mile, one-way walk to the top of Mt. Burdell, just keep going up on the main trail. At the summit of the mountain, the trail connects with the Mt. Burdell Open Space trail system.

Olompali was the site of a large Indian village for hundreds of years. It is believed to have been an important trading center. In 1579, Francis Drake and his ship the *Golden Hinde* arrived at the shores of Marin. The exact location of Drake's landing and placement of the brass plate proclaiming this new land for England are still debated. Great excitement was generated during an archaeological dig at Olompali in 1974 when a silver sixpence coin that dated to the Drake era was discovered. A coin of this type was reportedly affixed to the plate of brass left by Drake.

Local Indians built an adobe at Olompali in the 1820s. They had learned how to make adobe bricks at the nearby missions. Then in 1836, the original adobe was dismantled and the bricks were used to build a larger adobe for their Miwok leader, Camillo Ynitia. Portions of this adobe still stand today.

Olompali was given to Camillo Ynitia in 1843 by the Mexican Government. He was the only Indian in Marin to receive a land grant. Ynitia's adobe was the site of the only battle of the Bear Flag Revolt (1846) in which there were casualties. Three U.S. citizens were being held prisoner there by Mexicans. Mary Todd Lincoln's nephew, William Todd, who was the designer of the Bear Flag that became the California State flag, was reported to be one of the prisoners. During the skirmish, the U.S. prisoners were rescued.

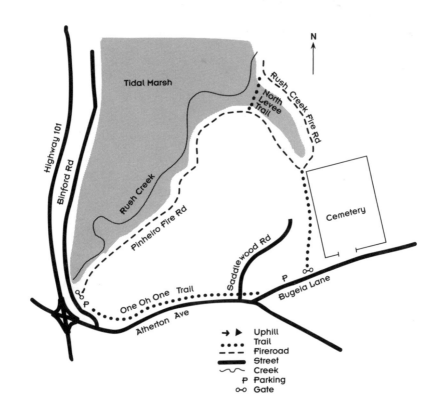

Rush Creek
Marin Open Space District

ACCESS: Binford Road, off Atherton Avenue

POINTS OF INTEREST: Birds and wildflowers

DISTANCE: Pinheiro Fire Road (one way): 1.5 miles
Rush Creek–North Levee–Pinheiro loop: 1 mile

DIFFICULTY: Easy

INFORMATION: Marin County Open Space
(415) 499-6405

Rush Creek
Marin Open Space District

Rush Creek Preserve, beside Highway 101 in Novato, offers an easy hiking trail with excellent bird-watching opportunities. Fire roads and trails weave alongside a large marsh that is prime habitat for a variety of birds. Bring binoculars, a bird identification book, and a spotting scope, if you have one.

The trails total about 3 miles, with the best views of the large marsh featured in the first 1.5 miles along the Pinheiro Fire Road. Generally done as an out-and-back walk along the Pinheiro Fire Road from the Binford Road entrance to the North Levee Trail, the hike can be made as long or short as you wish. The trails are mostly level. Winding along the edge of wooded hillsides, you pass though sections shaded by oaks trees and speckled with wildflowers.

A loop about 1 mile long can be walked around the marsh behind the cemetery. Continue on the Pinheiro Fire Road past the intersection with the North Levee Trail. The fire road narrows to a footpath. Turn left onto the Rush Creek Fire Road behind the cemetery. Oak trees line the Rush Creek Fire Road as it borders the small marsh. Turn left and cross the marsh on the narrow North Levee Trail. Rejoin the Pinheiro Fire Road for the return walk.

The marsh is often amass with white birds, which makes viewing easy and fun. Great white egrets and snowy egrets mingle with gulls and white pelicans. Great blue herons, black-neck stilts, and avocets are frequent visitors. Geese are also a common sight here, along with small waders such as yellowlegs, killdeers, and sandpipers. A large number of ducks can also be seen. With mallards as year-round residents, seasonal visitors include canvasbacks, pintails, widgeons, gadwalls, scaups, buffleheads, pied-billed grebes, and ruddy ducks.

Spring and summer feature sparrows darting in and out of shrubs, California towhees hopping about, black phoebes twittering from a fence wires, and belted kingfishers chattering as they fly by. Swallows skim and swoop in their typical feeding flight.

Rush Creek is named for an early landowner, Carl Peter Rush, who came to California during the gold rush and earned enough to purchase 406 acres of Rancho Novato in 1860.

About the Author

Tacy Dunham has been a hiker, adventure traveler, whitewater rafter, and Marin resident for most of her life. She has shared her outdoor experiences as a form of education, first as a teacher for eleven years, then as an author of Marin trail guide books, and currently as a newspaper columnist for the *Marin Independent Journal*.

Dunham's freelance writing began when she visited Yellowstone National Park still smoldering from the 1989 firestorm. Her descriptions from a naturalist's viewpoint were reprinted in newspapers and magazines anxious for firsthand accounts.

She writes for several adventure travel companies. Her globetrotting assignments help her discover exciting ways to experience the outdoors. She enjoys photographing unique landscape and wildlife in the polar regions. Her fascination with glaciers and icebergs first became clear on a trek to Alaska in 1995, which was followed by trips to photograph polar bears in Canada, penguins in Antarctica, and walrus in the high Arctic. She now balances her polar explorations with a variety of nature-oriented tours to both well-known and little known travel destinations.

Book Orders:

These books are available at bookstores or may be ordered directly from the publisher at the address below.

Exploring Marin Trails
by Tacy Dunham
© 2001, 96 pages, $9.
ISBN# 1-877967-08-4

Hiking Marin's Coast
by Tacy Dunham
© 2001, 96 pages, $9.
ISBN# 1-877967-09-2

Please add $3. per book for shipping and tax.
Cottonwood Press
610 El Arroyo Place
Novato, CA 94949
(415) 382-8590
cottonwoodpress4ca@hotmail.com